Isadora Vibes aka Katie Grant is a writer, the
stage her poetry in a more immersive, thea
performed a number of solo and ensemble sl
and Gothenburg. Artistic Director of the
guerrilla theatre company *Dada For Girls*,
new show based on the poems in this book. A scratch performance will debut at the Stockholm Fringe Festival in September 2018 before being developed into a tour-ready production for 2019. Isadora lives in Bristol and has two teenage children.

soak

Isadora Vibes

with Photography by Claudio Ahlers

Burning Eye

BurningEyeBooks
**Never Knowingly
Mainstream**

Copyright text © 2018 Isadora Vibes
Copyright in the photography © 2018 Claudio Ahlers

The author asserts the moral right under the Copyright, Designs and Patents Act 1988 to be identified as the author of this work.

All rights reserved. No part of this publication may be repro-duced, stored in a retrieval system, or transmitted, in any form or by any means without the prior written consent of the author, nor be otherwise circulated in any form of binding or cover other than that in which it is published and without a similar condition being imposed on the subsequent purchaser.

This edition published by Burning Eye Books 2018

www.burningeye.co.uk

@burningeyebooks

Burning Eye Books
15 West Hill, Portishead, BS20 6LG

ISBN 978-1-911570-51-6

Printed & bound by ImprintDigital.com, UK

soak

October 2019.

Dearest Liam

(Billy Elliott :)) x

Thank you for a wonderful evening and I hope you enjoy these words.

littered needles
to mend a hole
your soul awaits
a new calling
overseas — the question
answered
x

For Rufus, I&I and No.3

I feel all shadows of the universe multiplied deep inside my skin.
Virginia Woolf, Diary, 5 November 1931

CONTENTS

MONSTERS	13
PREPARATION	15
SKIN	17
PARTITION	19
DROWNING	21
LA VIE EN ROSE (CINQUAIN)	23
COLGATE	25
WASHING GRANDMA'S HAIR	27
SPILT/SPLIT	29
DNA	31
WEATHER REPORT	33
JAW	35
THREESOME	37
UNMADE	39
SIAMESE	41
GIFT	43
MEMORY GAME	45
AIRBRUSHED	47
JIGGLE GIRL	49
FETISH 1	51
POST-COITAL ETIQUETTE	53
WIRE WOOL	55
PEG FEED	57
BLACKBERRIES	59
CARVED	61
CATHARSIS	63

LADY V	65
BONES	67
WATCHING THE BIRDS	69
QUATRAIN	71
TEACHINGS OF THE FATHER	73
RUSH (ST MARY REDCLIFFE, 2012)	75
EASTER SUNDAY	77
REINCARNATION	79
SCRAPED	81
SCALP & SAUSAGE	83
FRAGMENTS OF A DAY (ONE VOICE)	84
TRISTESSE	89
KEYHOLE	91
COLD SHOULDER	93
SOUP 1 (NEW YEAR'S DAY)	94
SOUP 2 (FOUR YEARS EARLIER)	95
GHERKINS	97
PUNK SKY (STOKES CROFT)	99
ARBORETUM	101
TOMB	103
BRANCHES OF SKY	105

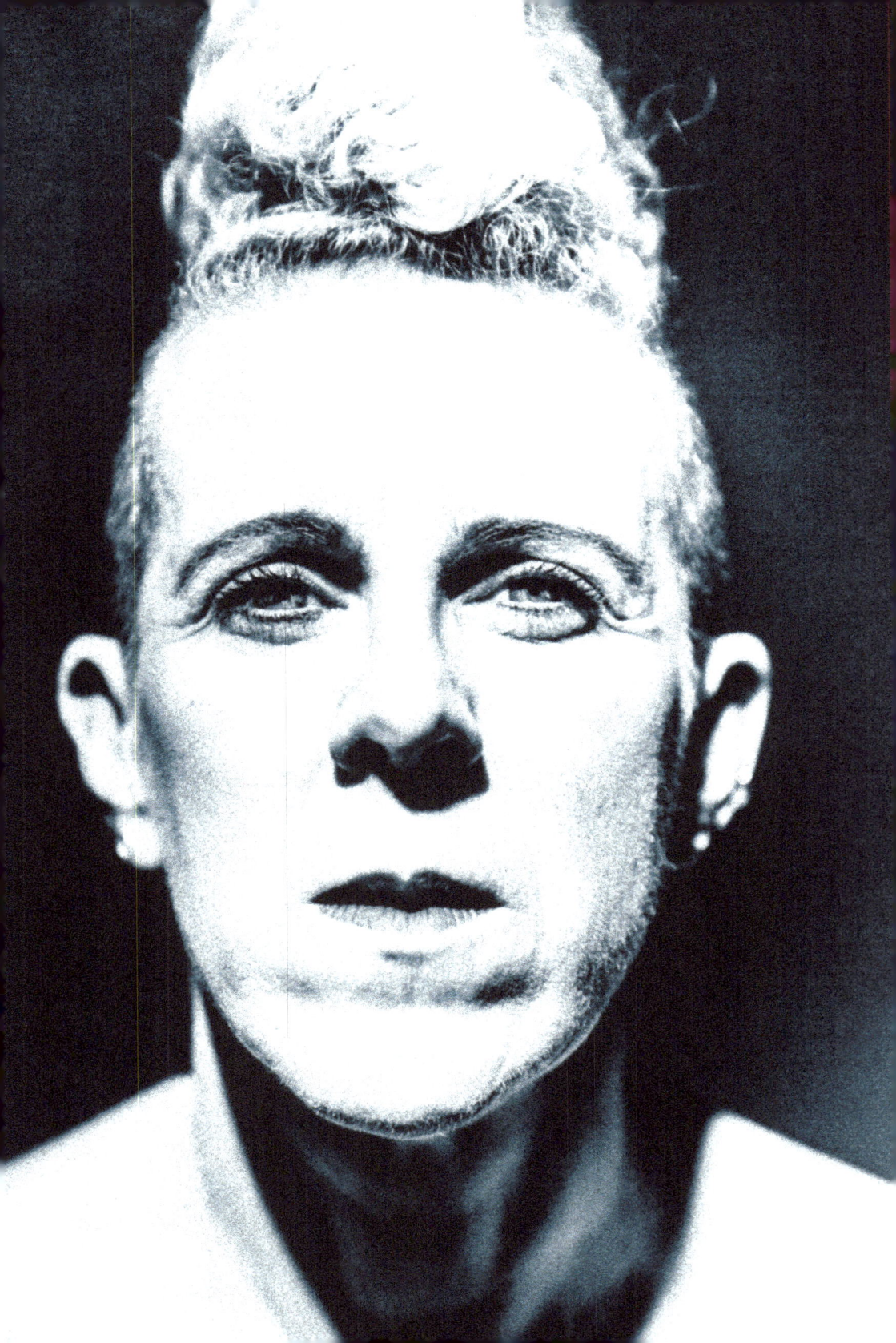

MONSTERS

When I was young
My father kept me safe
From things that lived under the bed
And snapped at heels left dangling out of sheets
And lashing tongues that poked and spat
As I ran past and fled
Down corridors of gorgon-headed snakelike fiends
With barbs of poison reaching out to strike and puncture
Youthful skin. And blackened deadly-nightshade-purple
Spikes on either side to dodge as I ran panting, breathless, switched
on light.

Now I am grown and live alone
There is no guide to tell me where and when to hide.
The monsters all wear suits and ties
And coat their tongues in plausible lies.
Telling me that all will be lovely, absolutely fine,
And what's your problem?
We just need time. And I will be there when I say
And I will love you every day.
And every sun that rises
In the sky we will watch and call our own.
Our children fair will be well known.
They will enthral and conquer all
In world of shiny, glittering stars;
No monsters now lurk in the dark.

But underneath the well-cut suits
Are tails that only can be seen
By those who know and once have been
Caught by monsters just like these,
Snatched and thrown to grassy stair,
Left to struggle unaware,
No daddy there to hear their cry
Or dry the salty tears of fear.
So listen, dears – be wary, hide.
The monsters live, they never die.

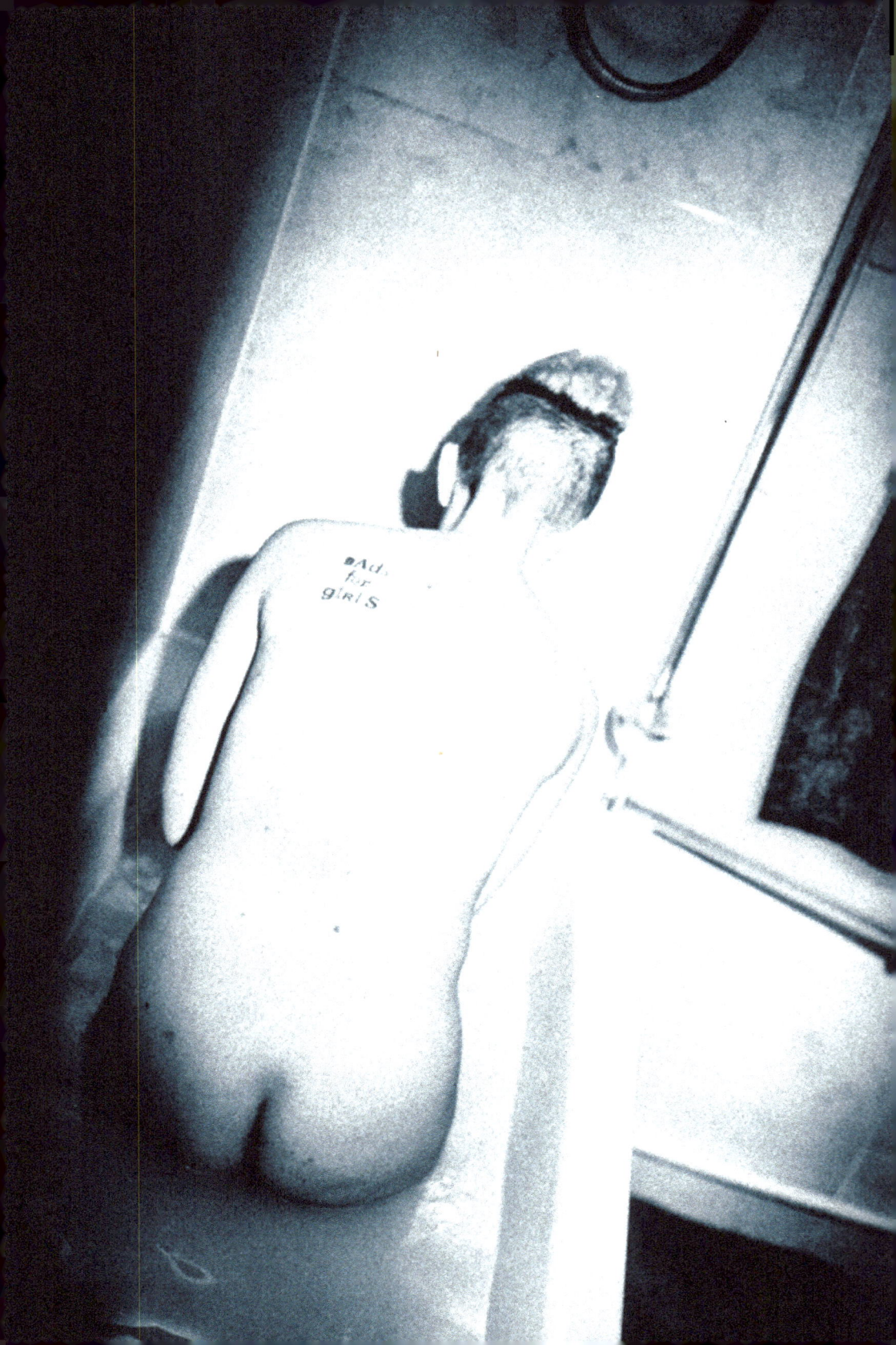

PREPARATION

I wash.
I pluck.
I sit.
I shit.
I bathe.
I shave.
I dry.
I try.
I ask you
What you like
Down there.
How much hair?
A lot? A little?
Or completely bare.
You pause for thought,
Then text appears.
A little, you say.
Ah – that's OK.
But what does it mean?
Bed is ready, sheets are clean.
Pillows plumped and duvet smoothed.
Teeth are brushed and knickers moved.
My stash of erotica hidden away,
Books I keep for a rainy day.
I dress, like a doll.
In black with trim.
I wonder – will it impress him?
Will he notice the little things?
I think about my crotch – it stings.
I curse this female preparation
To take a chance on fornication.
The doorbell goes –
I adjust a rose
And trip down stair
To find you
Standing
There.

SKIN

My favourite place to write is on your skin.

In darkness dim, you sprawl – expansive blank of parchment tall –
longing for the nourishment only this ink brings.

Silhouetted against this bed – a shadowed hand is raised to drape
    across your contoured chest –
the perfect desk.

Night curtain falls – a sheer veneer of blackened hue.
I climb aboard you.
Weightless now I touch, caress your furrowed brow,

Trace plump lips with quill; words drip and spill.
A sacramental penance paid to priest in languid scrawl.
Visibly this ink appears confessing silent sin.

Fragmented, revealing, in calligraphic swirl:
A name, a place, a time, a face.
What guilt-fuelled guile – in sleep you smile.

Ignorance is bliss.

Full stop. A kiss.

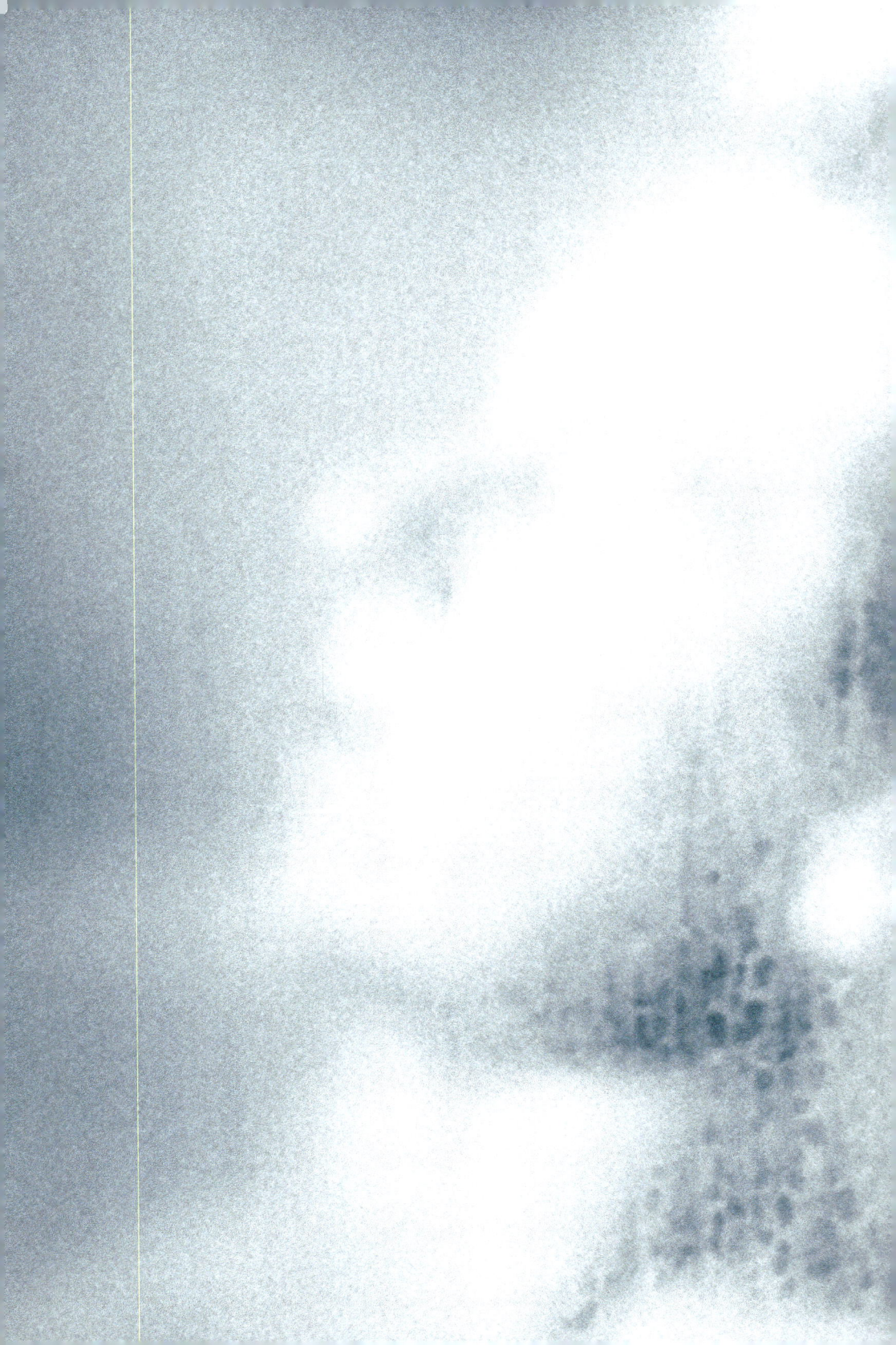

PARTITION

The hands of a goddess are small, he said.
Entwined in armoury of curls
Hauled from the well of a fathom
Too deep to be charted.

Words of ancient times have scored our sleep,
Deep lines between this love
Caulking the longest seam;
My pitch is blacker.

Each dream is filled with gods, she said.
Screaming dry-tongued demons
Licking us inside and out
As coracle capsizes.

DROWNING

water
aqua
natal
deluge
skimming
trimming
skin

in shallow space
we suck and duck
hard tiles imprison
flesh-toned fuck
forced to slip and drip on blue-chipped toe tip
tugging rub to lip

sud soak poking
juddered cheek
in porcelain slap back
banged up sleek
licked to slick by rib tongue taut ridge porn stick
hydrostatic click

blind blue battered
drum thud thrum
glued pink purple
statical numb
pawed to pink pained sky straining rise to gulp
coral stem palm pulp

I fear I may drown
mouth is full and ripe with you
flesh ready pulse of male
wet with all the liquid one can swallow
no room for air
earth or fire

only water

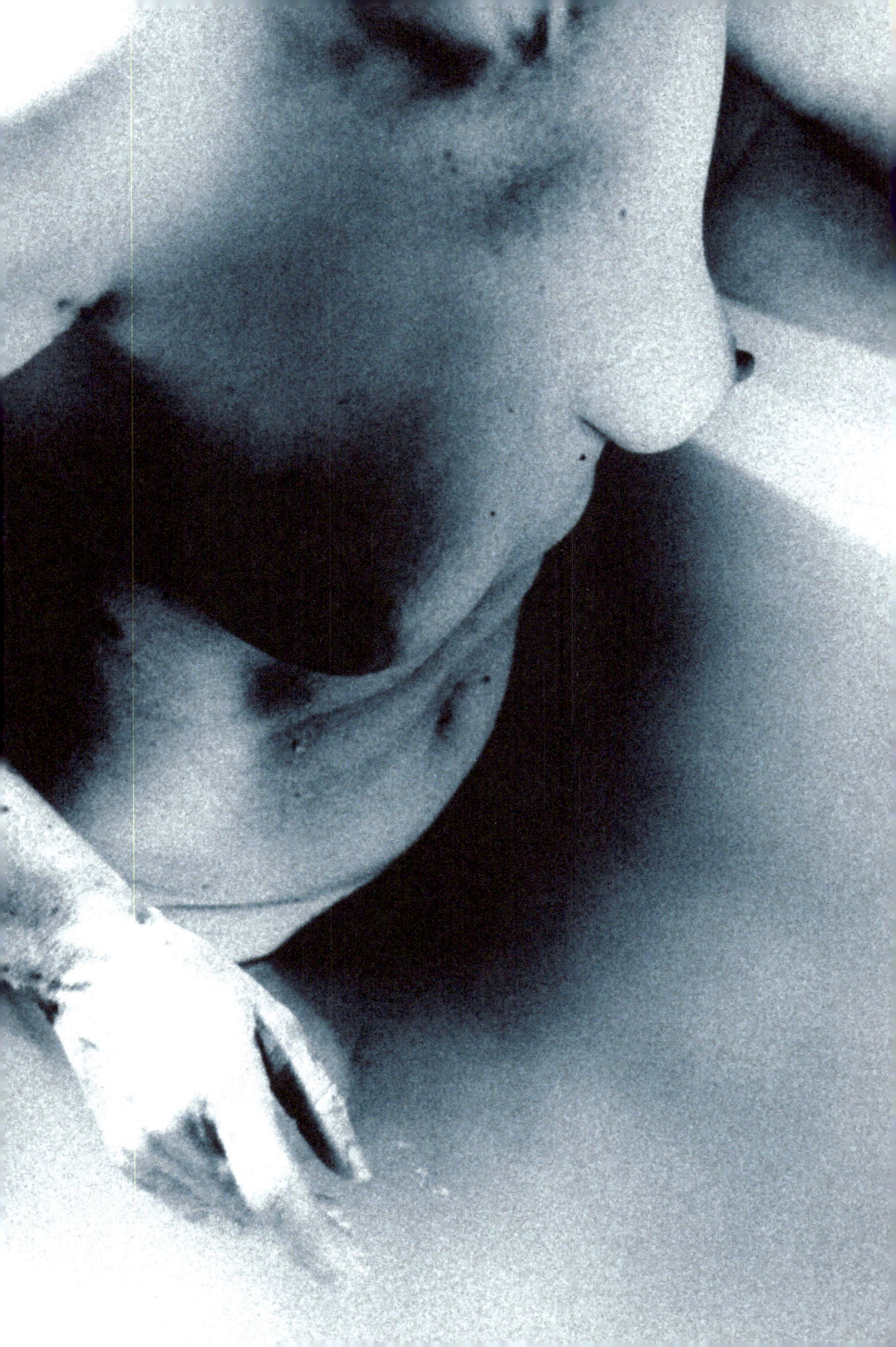

LA VIE EN ROSE (CINQUAIN)

scarlet
a sudden loss
blossoming
vermilion petals
penetrate

claret
pigmentation dares
to brush against
a skin palette
redrawn

cardinal
chromosomal error
clotting sin
the night
clawing

carmine
wine-stained entry
gashing spill
recalling
poppies

ruby
lip pound gore
spotting silk
the soak of it
gutting

COLGATE

you have left the cap off again
but instead of squeezing
fudge mint ooze
onto side of sink
there is a deliberation
doppelgänger-thin
the space between
message to him
that I am categorically
never going to get back
together and yet
the symmetry
of this twinned trail
sluggishly mint
leaves a double white
no parking sparkle
on the vinyl squares
of a promise
you have not kept
gingerly stepping
to empty myself
the smudge of your demise
staining hem

never again

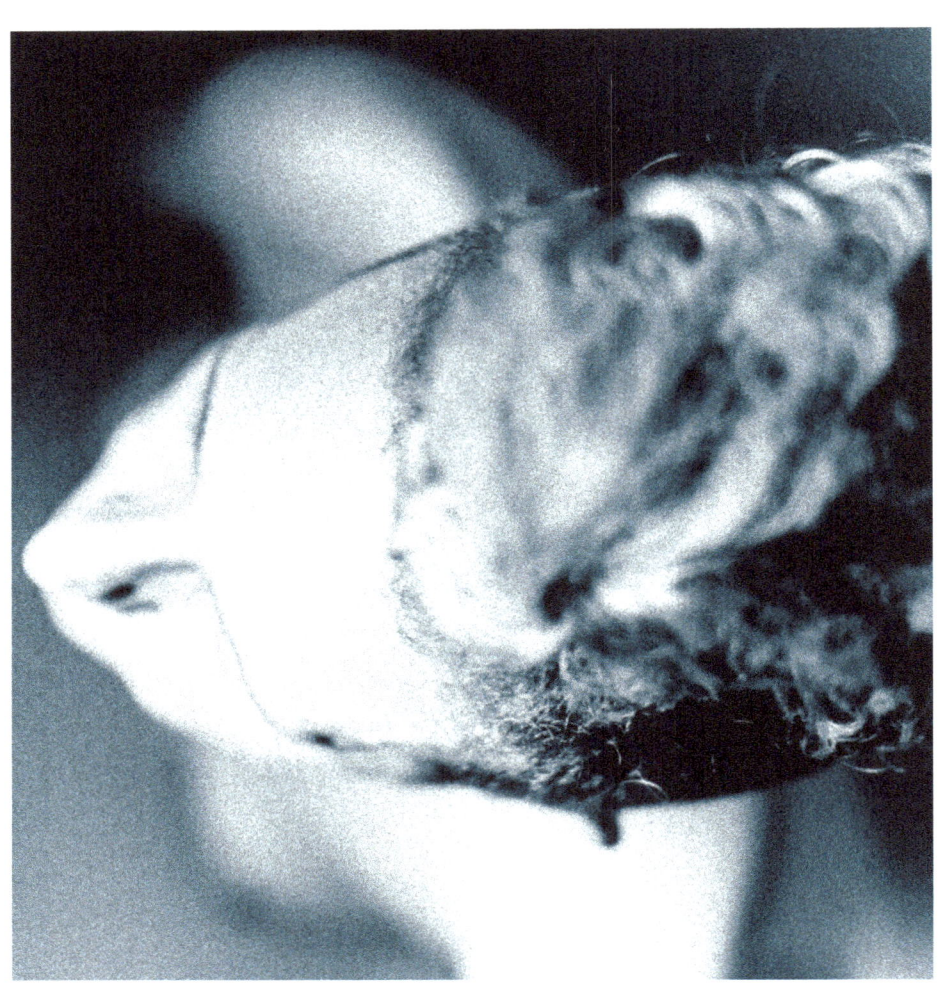

WASHING GRANDMA'S HAIR

fragile like a child
she rests bare flesh
against this cold
metallic iron space
the water spilling, slopping
echoing then stopping
tap is gushing, rushing as
on bended knee she lowers
shrunken frame
slightly strained in pain
she bends to be baptised
as I, in role of priest
reach to scoop
warm water
nape of neck still brown
from sunny climes
in Dionysos, older times
her leg a legend
some might say
that never quite recovered
pausing now
I soothe her brow
head is bowed
the sparse spun silver
straight shafts bleached
by passing years
her fears and tears
a testament to youth
and crowning glory snatched away
by careless driver
shocked but lucky still
this snowy thatch is soft to touch
full cup saturating
wincing, water not quite right
she reaches up, her sunspot hands
to hold mine tight
our spirits merge and soar
we are as one behind closed door

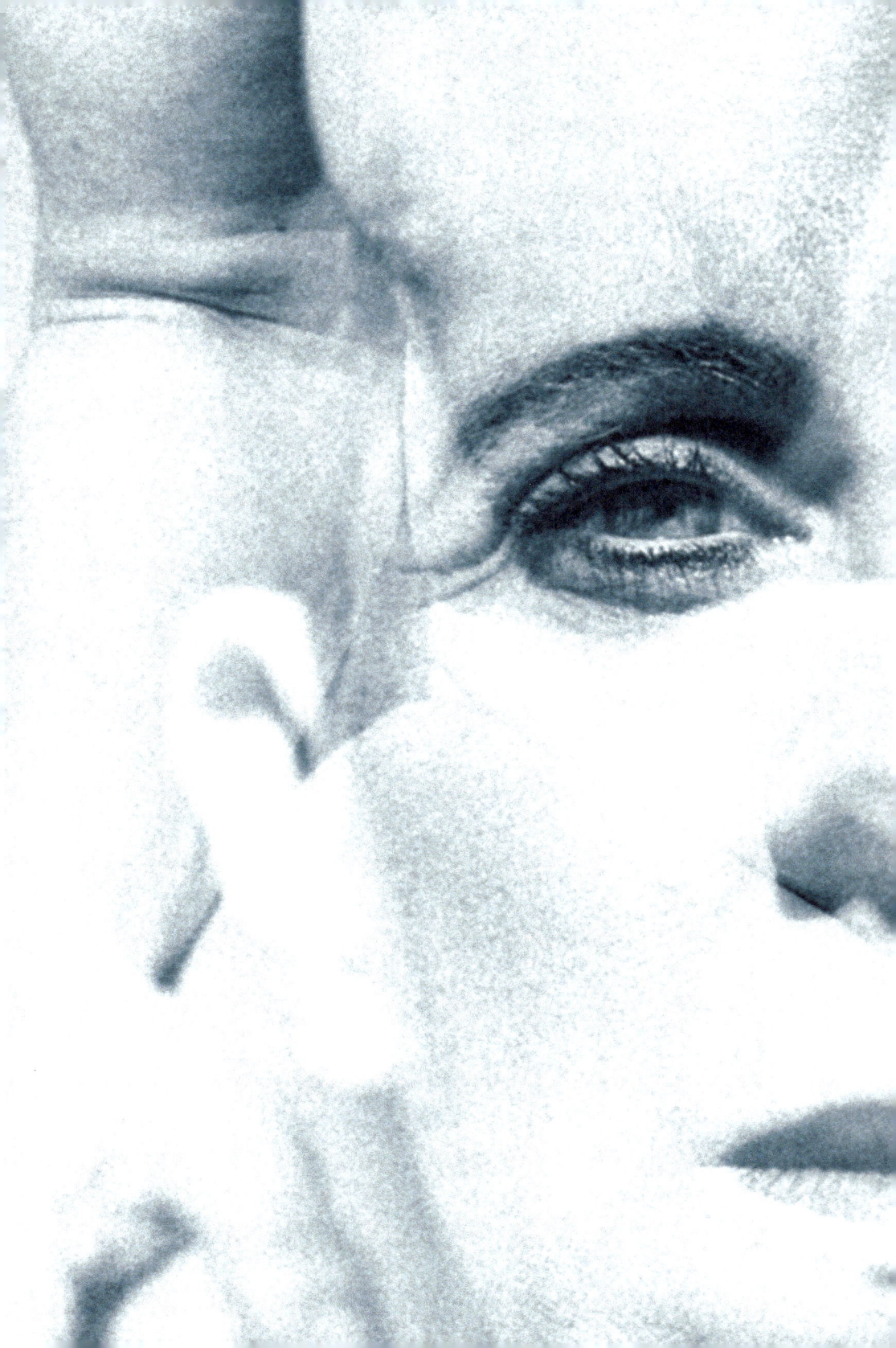

SPILT/SPLIT

the remnants of torn
silting skin

we filter dark desire

fermenting tears
into pooled pillars

salt of sorrow
solidifies

as lies seep into slumber

a foul residue
stains sweet dreams

the nightmare seducing
each orifice

into split-seamed
sorrowful sin

DNA

Afterwards, I do not wash
but tiptoe, trot to toilet, palm protector
catching all that you have lost.
Lick from fingers salted stain of predawn buck –
alarm has interrupted frantic clutch to fuck
and now the day is crowding;
loud cacophony of overzealous choral wow.
Children stir and sneak to ask if it is time to get up now.
The damp of you is there –
an intermittent drip and spill.
I smell the male of all I cannot be.
Outwardly I am still me and yet inside a forest jungle grows.
Heady musk of trust divulged and stored, where no one else can go.
I will this sticky place to stay where I have placed it
and yet soon I fear it, then you, then I will fade away.
Evaporate.
Swimming, sluicing through from early train to meeting,
nihilistic tweeting, greeting – salvaged pride still flushed from night of
    over-fucking love.
By evening cotton swab is dry.
I do not cry or mourn the loss of misspent bliss – remainder of a kiss.
Silently I wipe this salted stain of DNA, unsure of what to say.
Reeling ever closer to my middle age,
we roll as one togetherness – in linen-covered night.

WEATHER REPORT

armageddon
we seek refuge
in blue

JAW

Bone.
The one I use to speak with, say things,
Fixed inside my head to yawn when bored, is sore.
Strained and raw.
Pleased, I do believe, I have this soreness to remember.
Steamed-up windows – metallic box,
Forgetting child locks.
Back seat prison – entered bare.
We step through hidden door.
You ask to take a look.
I could see your eyes half open, veiled in curtain
Thick with lust – fixated on this mouth.
I could have been saying anything.
Reciting tables, quotes from theatre,
Red-top news and scandal.
Paper. Weak. Thin crackered jokes.
Last smoke trampled,
Trodden into dust.
This trust – thrown from window.
As you ask politely, I pull down.
Lay my dignity on a knife-edge.
A tightrope stretched
Between skyscraper you and a chasm so deep.
With eyes stitched open – I feel cheap.
In a good way, of course.
How many women have opened their mouths to take in this view?
Vertiginous, new.
And yet, as we dance, I sense a new balance
My head is forced.
You clutch each curl and way below I smile for I can do this.
Without regret, remorse.
Of course, I know what others may think.
With knowing, nudging woman wink
They say I sell myself.
Trading femininity, sacrificing loyalty
For a liquid, salty supper.
I beg to disagree.
I chose this.
I wanted to.
This moment sets me free.

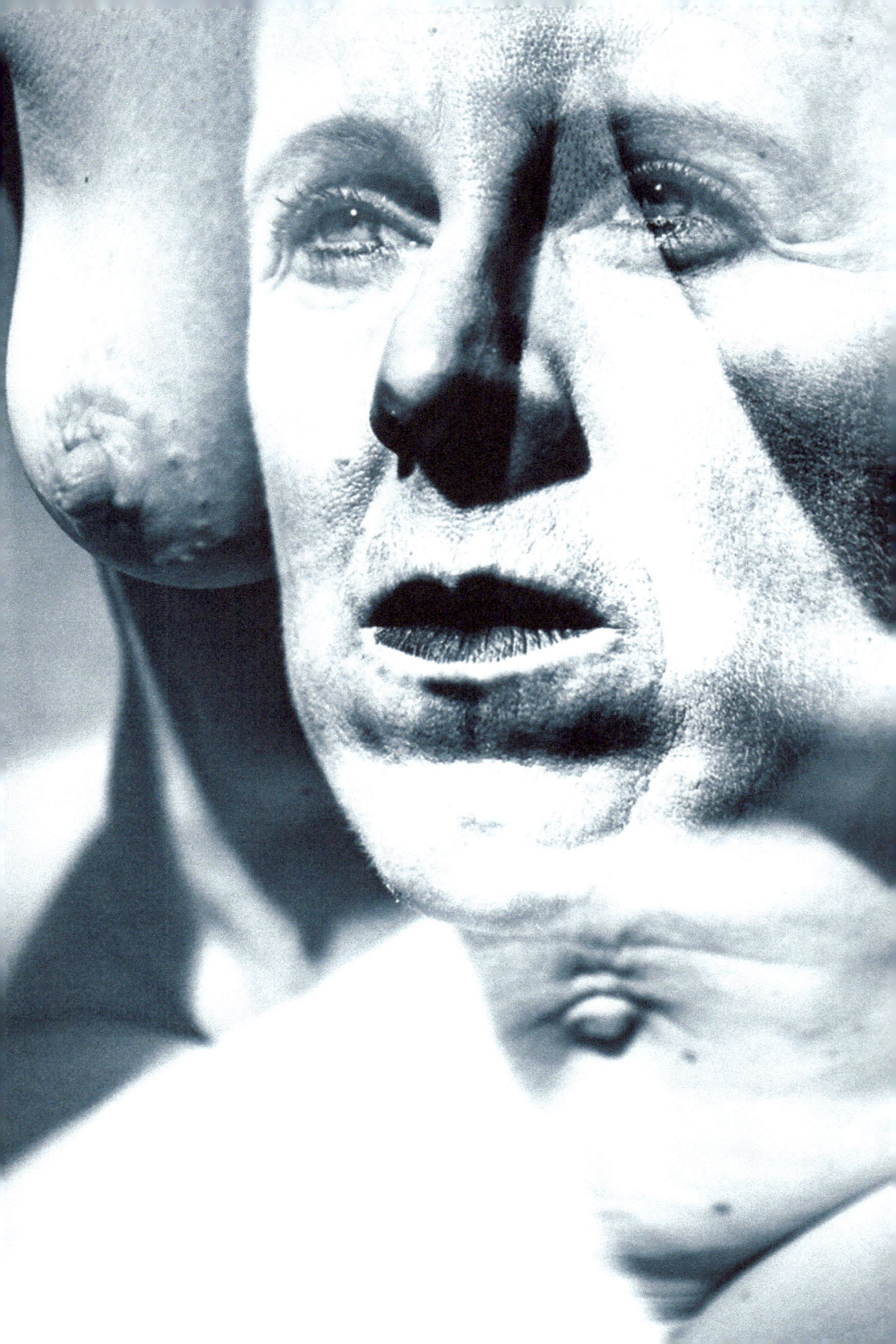

THREESOME

Slow – this distillation
As unfamiliar tongue
Rolls and plays into
Dip and tuck
Swelled by other juices
The buck and bush of this lush heat
Incites the night to charge.
As linen loosens, mouth and teeth
Speak a new language.
Biblical promises crumble in lust
And we are not sorry.
Brain-buzzed bravery is capped.
Like a medal, you pin yourself
Onto goose-gripped flesh –
Wrestle each curve
Deeper into diamond –
The hinterland of dawn
Lies far from these suburban shores
And all is sweat and butter.
Clench crushing folds
Engulfed into mould –
Two become three and still
This is not enough.
By kitten pant and whisper,
You twist and tug for more.
My hand too small for your puppetry,
I fear fracture, yet cannot stop.
Locs trapped under pale shoulders,
We become giant,
Six-armed, six-legged, supersonic.
Held to ransom, desperate
Breath escapes,
Sticking to ribs like feathers.
We freeze as residue dries,
Cries subside as you slip
Snugly into diamond.
4am is a shudder of lost.
Twice you rest.
Twice you test my valour.
Sinking deep into passive
Sleep is a shared blessing.
We hold tight to the equation.

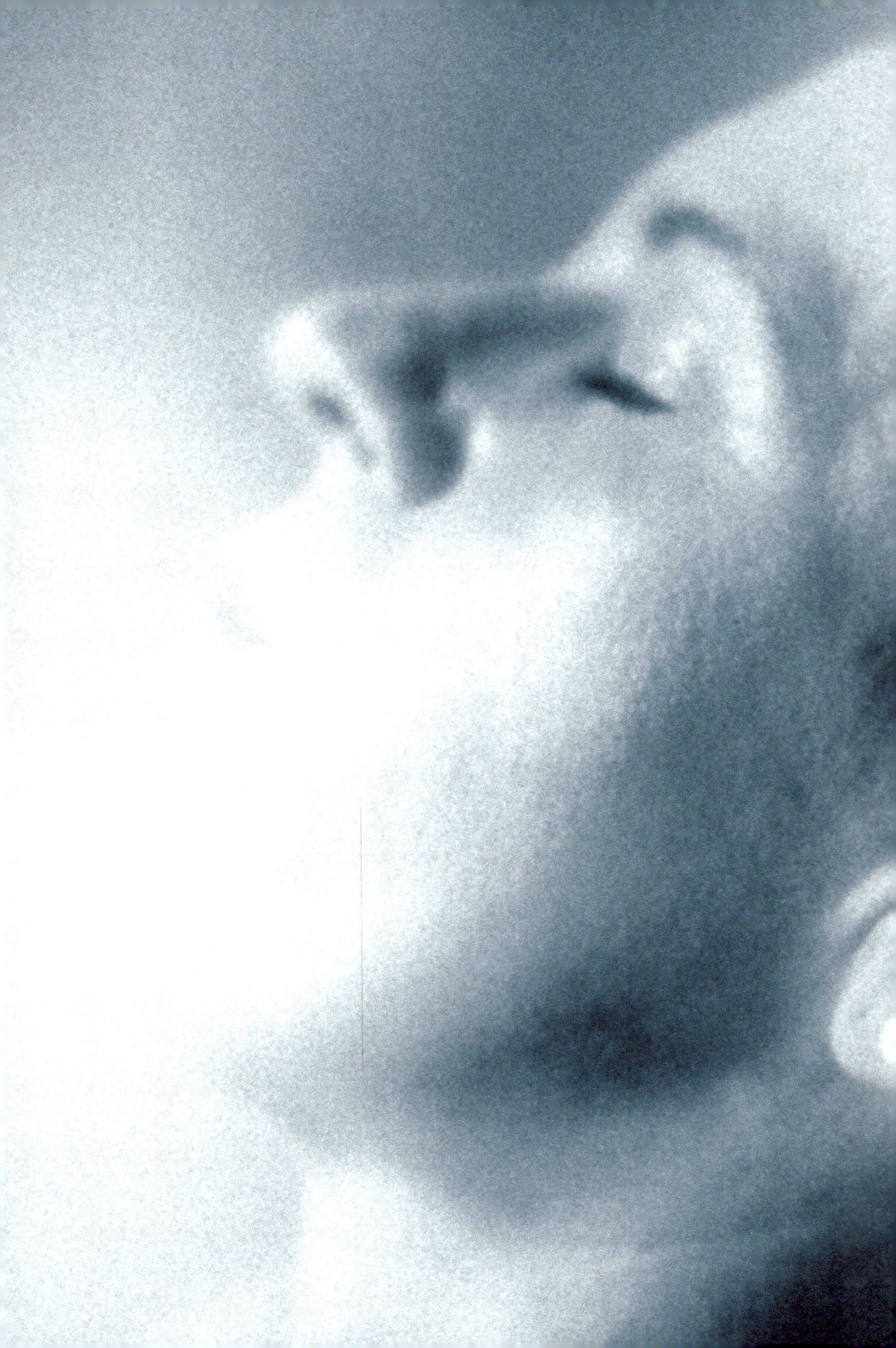

UNMADE

This bed is island –
Archipelago.
Floating free – no strings to tie.
Wave to me as you pass by.

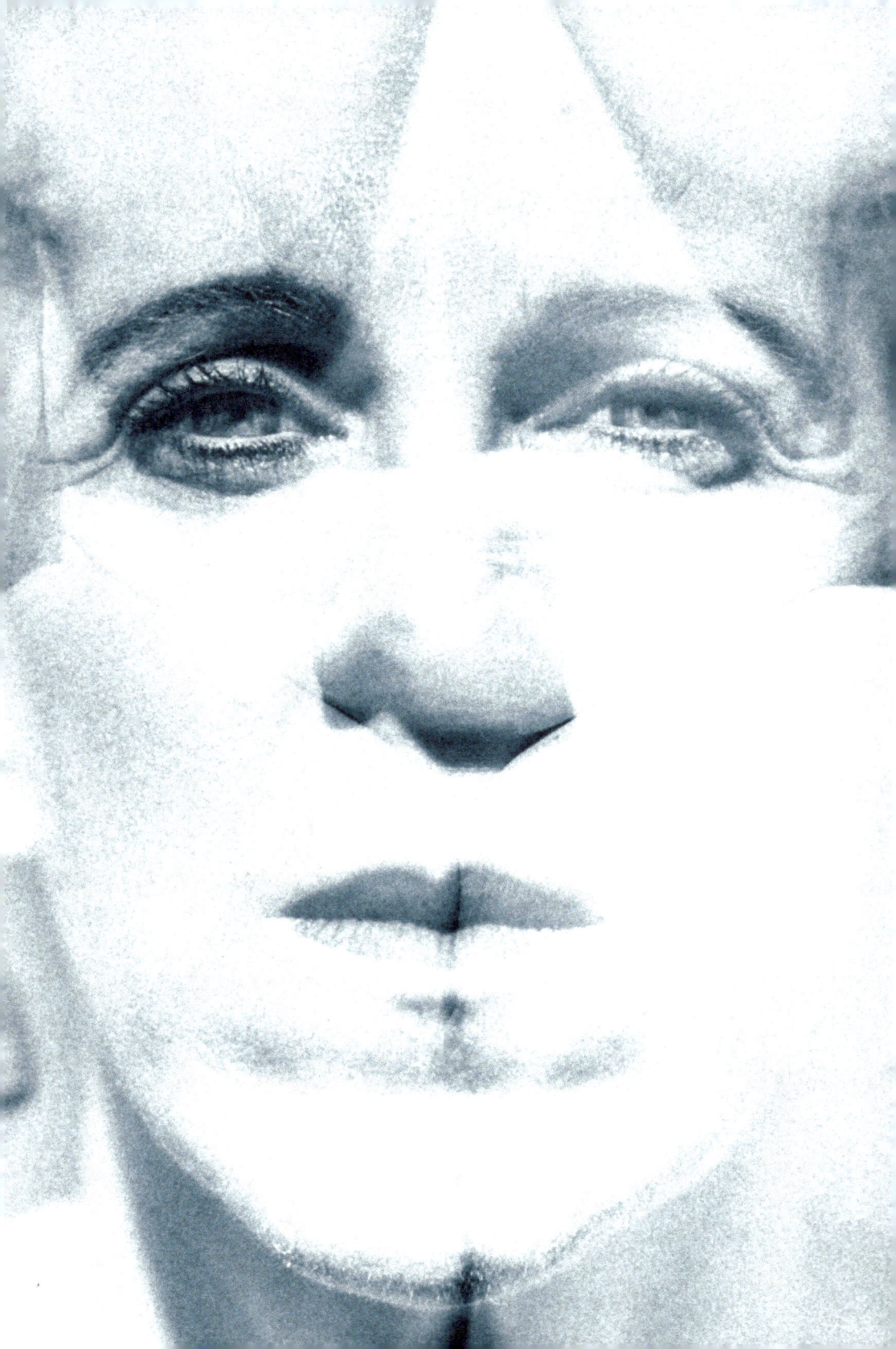

SIAMESE

the other me is whispering
deep in my ear
her long tongue
unravelling like liquorice
sucking out the marrow
secretion of nights spent
with fingers
entwined in wet sheets
and silent stifled cries
the nectar of this sticky ruin
cradles tongue in blissful
bee-stung shame

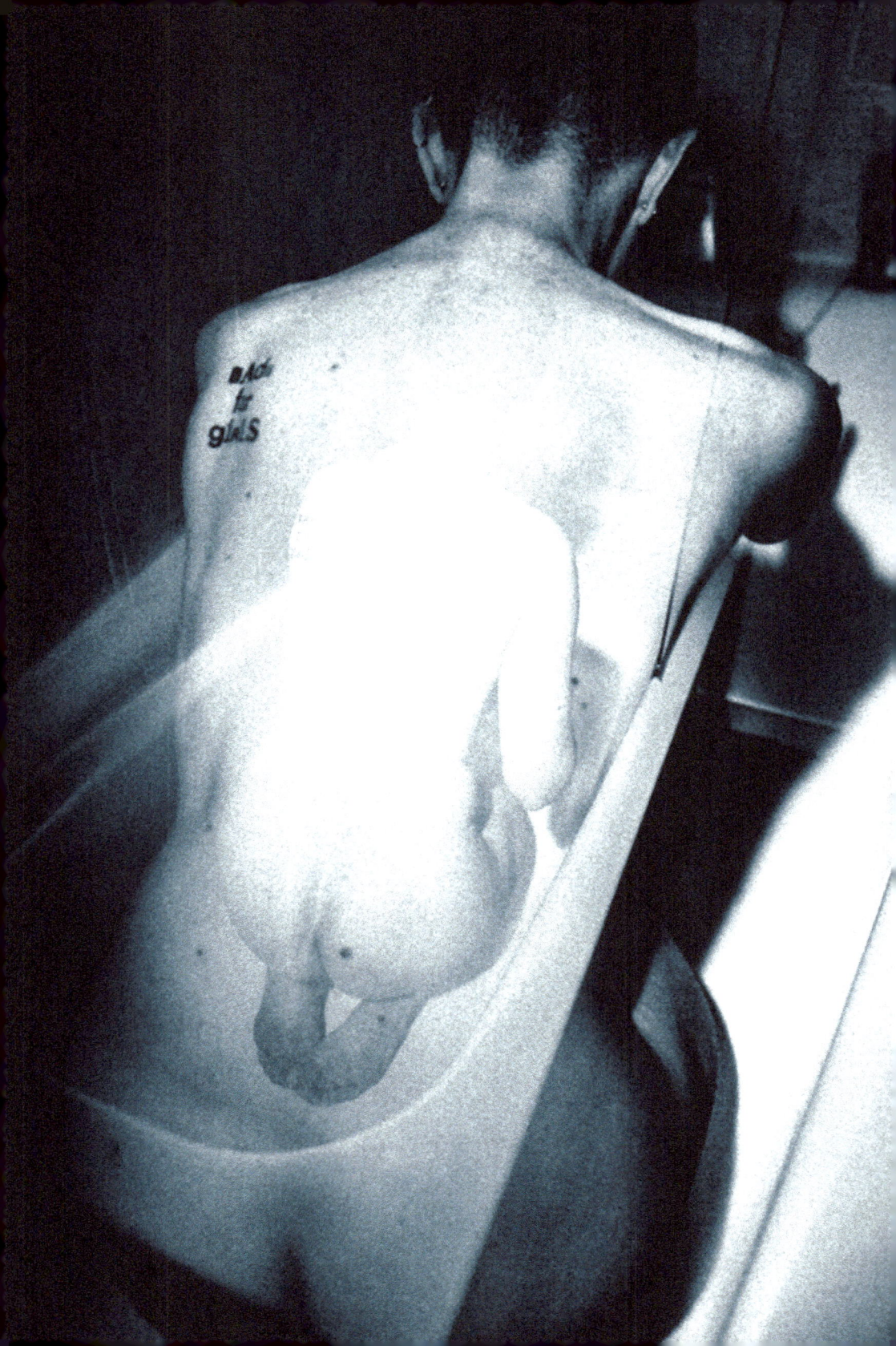

GIFT

I shall present myself
Gift-wrapped again
Just like the first time
Although now, of course
Some damage has occurred
Mainly around the eyes
And naturally my thighs are not as you left them
Although if you narrow gaze
The sight could still be pleasing
And may possibly
Cause you to rise
Which will help, of course
After all, isn't that the surprise
Inside that you still find me
Enough.

I shall temper response
Knowing that this
Is what you want
And indeed not look into your eyes
At your request I have
Turned myself away
Raising all fours on knees that
Cannot take the strain anymore
Yet still push back
Against the force of this
Unwanted repellent push
As dry lips strain
To take the full length
Of a life spent
Trying.

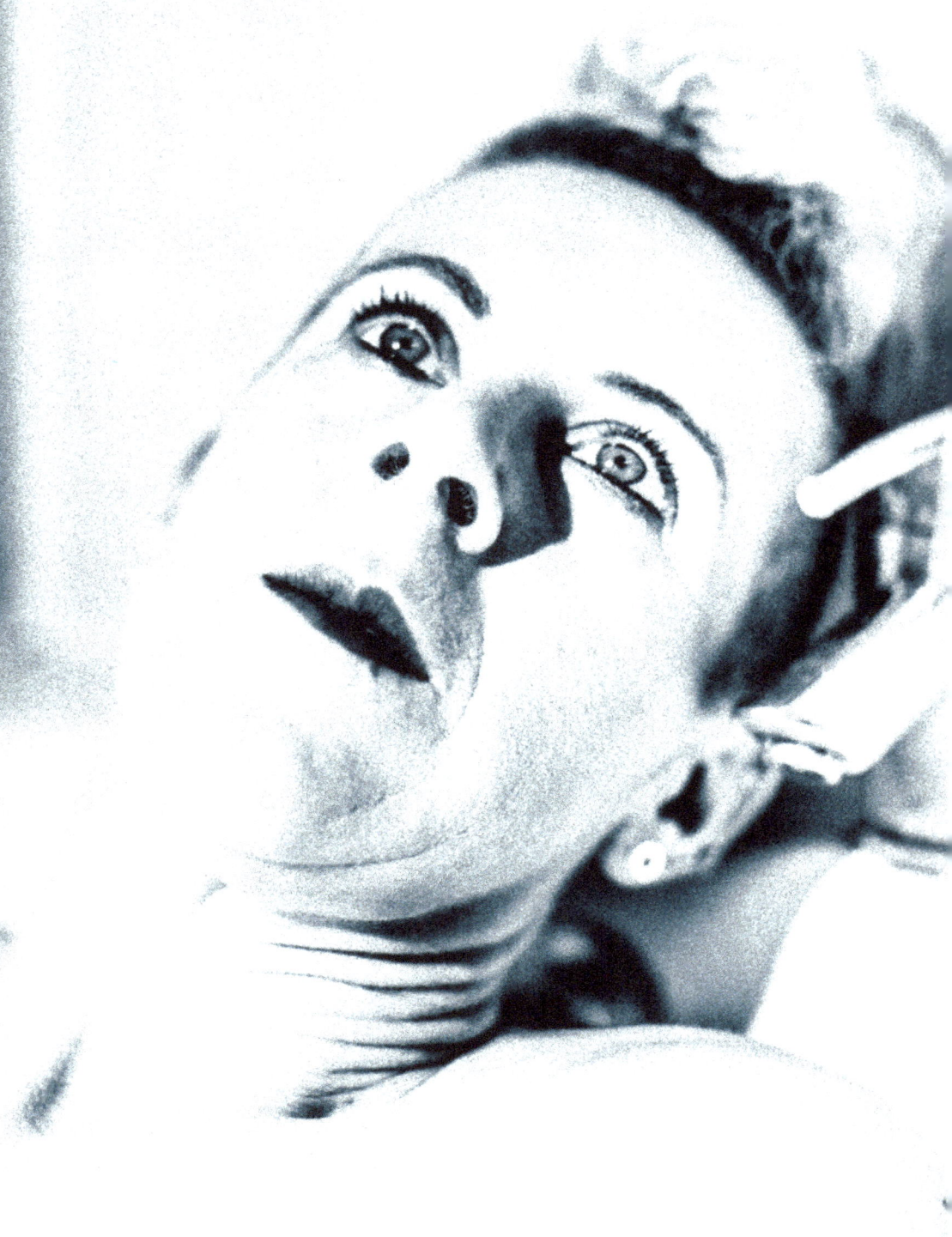

MEMORY GAME

I remember the carpet.
Blue with a brown fleck.
Face down the cards lay,
Boxed into square.
As we – kneel-grooved,
Our jumpered elbows pressed,
Peering intently,
Desperate to remember
Each pattern and pair.
She was not there.
All we had was flat-packed
Dog-eared entertainment.
Egg and chips arrived,
Garnished by a stray beagle hair.
The room made me retch
And dash to tight-bound seat
Gagged by American Tan.
Pretty Polly had left long ago.
Together we faced this
Challenge to remember.
Teapot, telephone, bluebird, biscuit.
Two years, two months and seventeen days,
I deserved this victory.
As Wagon Wheels
Melted in milk,
Twinned we bridge the afternoon.
Awaiting rescue.

AIRBRUSHED

On the shelf she can just about reach
If she stands on the tips of her high-top
Plastic hot-to-trot trainers she can see
The other women she wants to be,
This eight-year-old beauty
Patting her perfection.
She turns and asks me,
How old is Kylie?
I reply she is my age.
No – she gasps – really?
Yes, I say as finger lingers
On pop princess's tawny thigh.
I sigh.
Actually – she is older,
I continue, bolder,
Only to be met with derision.
The sin of this confession
Is not met with agreement
As she turns attention back to Ms Minogue,
Smouldering – shot to precision.
My decision to be true
Is not stemming the flow of questions.
How is that so?
I see her pause – calculating,
Recalibrating understanding
As she looks back at me,
Her mother at forty-three.

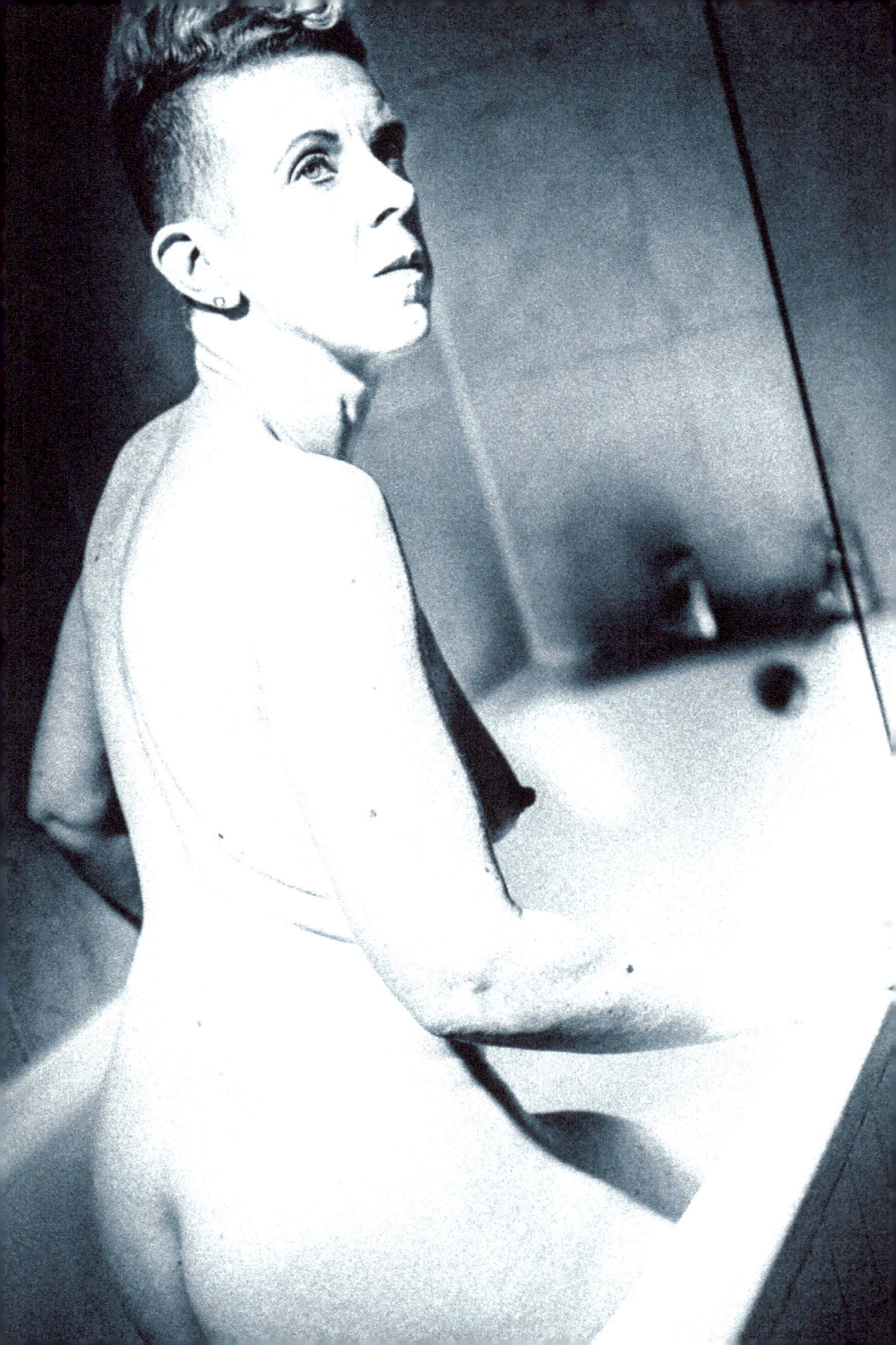

JIGGLE GIRL

Let us not despise the jiggle girl
As, after all, she has a talent and a place
With her very own channel and face
Turned away from camera.
All we see is sheer frivolity.
As 4am peaks into starry infinity
She and her sister provide the only
Decent company in a night that has
Once again left a stain of unfulfilled
On a carpet that really does need
A deep-down steam clean –
Jiggle girl is queen,
Contorting her curves into jolly shapes.
Her biggest mistake was surgery.
Does she not regret the decision
To go larger than life? And now,
As the night line switches its tone,
Phone begins to sag, as elbow
Bruised from digital contortions
Droops to allow her a moment of rest,
To sit, have a drink, smoke a fag.
Tomorrow she'll be somebody else's
Solitary, late-night shag.

FETISH 1

suckled
double-breasted matriarchs
slaver for attention
Rubenesque – their pungent flesh
flayed into pink whipped strip
from a distance – we are safe
enslaved like them
by doppelgänger pleasure
measured in our gaze
a French maid sashays
serving cappuccino cup cake
his fishnets chafe
carrying the weight
of a dry and heavy bone

POST-COITAL ETIQUETTE

You can bet, when it's over,
He'll fancy a fag or consider the fact he's forgotten to top up the gas.
Recall in his mind the girl he met at the club last night – the music was shite
Still, she didn't look bad in the neon green, could he bear to be seen bending over revealing a hairless hole.
The cellulite offset by Primark-trimmed lips – she was smelling of Impulse and yesterday's chips.
Porn style unwound in his Fray Bentos mind, she was gagging for air as the lollipop ram got stuck in her hair.
Punish her quick, she was begging for meat from a half-mast squish-boned dick-fucked cheat.
Pussy breath lingers, he mints up his tongue, erases the number she punched in so young.
Home now. He tiptoes. Sweat turning cold.
Congealing, revealing – turns over to hold.
Her body too old to be seen in the light.

Good night.

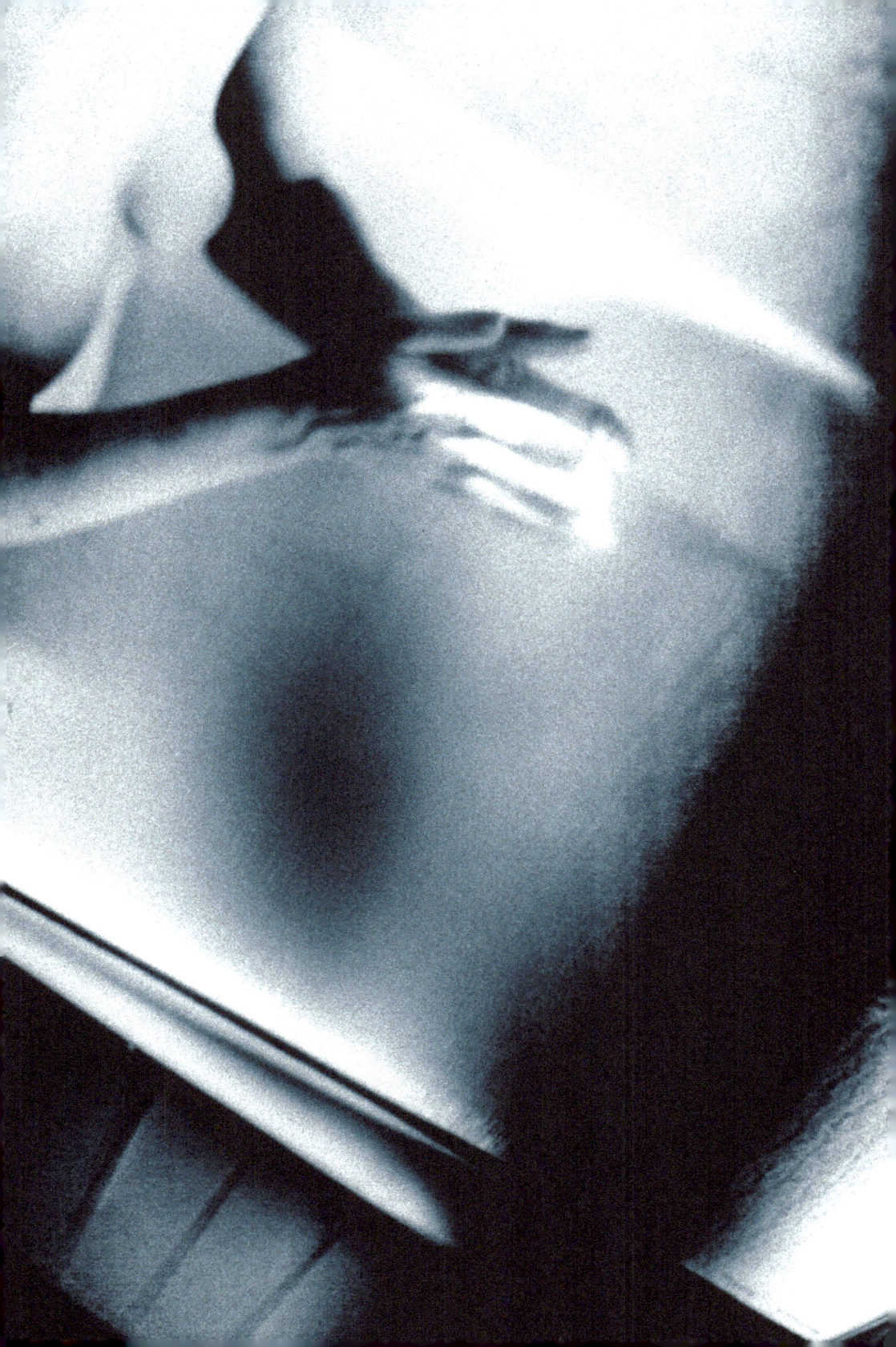

WIRE WOOL

I can never get you clean enough.
In slipper morning manic
Indulging the precarious,
We straddle porcelain,
Me and the rabbit.
Straining necks to check
Meringue-stiff stucco,
Egg white whiskered.
This is not the view we wished for,
A rusty plug hole whore.
My Hitchcock retrospective
Dizzy with psychobabble.
Down there all is wet and slick,
Loose gloop staining all,
Clothed yet insecure –
For a second… balance falters.
Imagine the catastrophe,
Alone and foetally deprived,
Split skull bleeding into tap
Flushed away with the coffee dregs,
Metallic stopper – silenced.

PEG FEED

marked in symmetry
her ungloved reach
pawing the air
parting molecular cool
until soft fingers
relieved in bone
find cloud-punctured knuckles
savouring the empty
equality of digits
separated
inch by inch
this light of chance
framed in chiaroscuro
fitting – the final wave
of anorexic sorrow
as silence
masking palm
permits one final
absolute commitment
to denial

BLACKBERRIES

I name this day as Mrs Dalloway
by virtue of the fact that on waking
I am no longer intact.
And the dawn is more oppressive than an army of thought police.
Sniper-driven, craning necks to spy the likes of I.
Guilty as charged, restricting happiness
    like a throttled bird, breath held before flight.
The night brings relief, as mind is permitted
    to swoop and soar into subconscious winged thought.
They say that sleep cements bad memories and so
I regret the indulgence of rest in earlier years.
Too ignorant to know of somnambulistic damage done.
And so I marvel at the courage it might take to just stop this life in its prime.
After all my chores are complete and bed begs me back to its muffled
    ear-dulled feathered cool.
The walls are friends to whisper and confide that all is not right or will
    not be.
You see how easy it might seem to slip into comatose infancy.
As knives are washed and dried, the moment to gore passes.
But in this knowledge is the pain of not eating the blackberries
that others are picking, as the morning stretches into infinity.

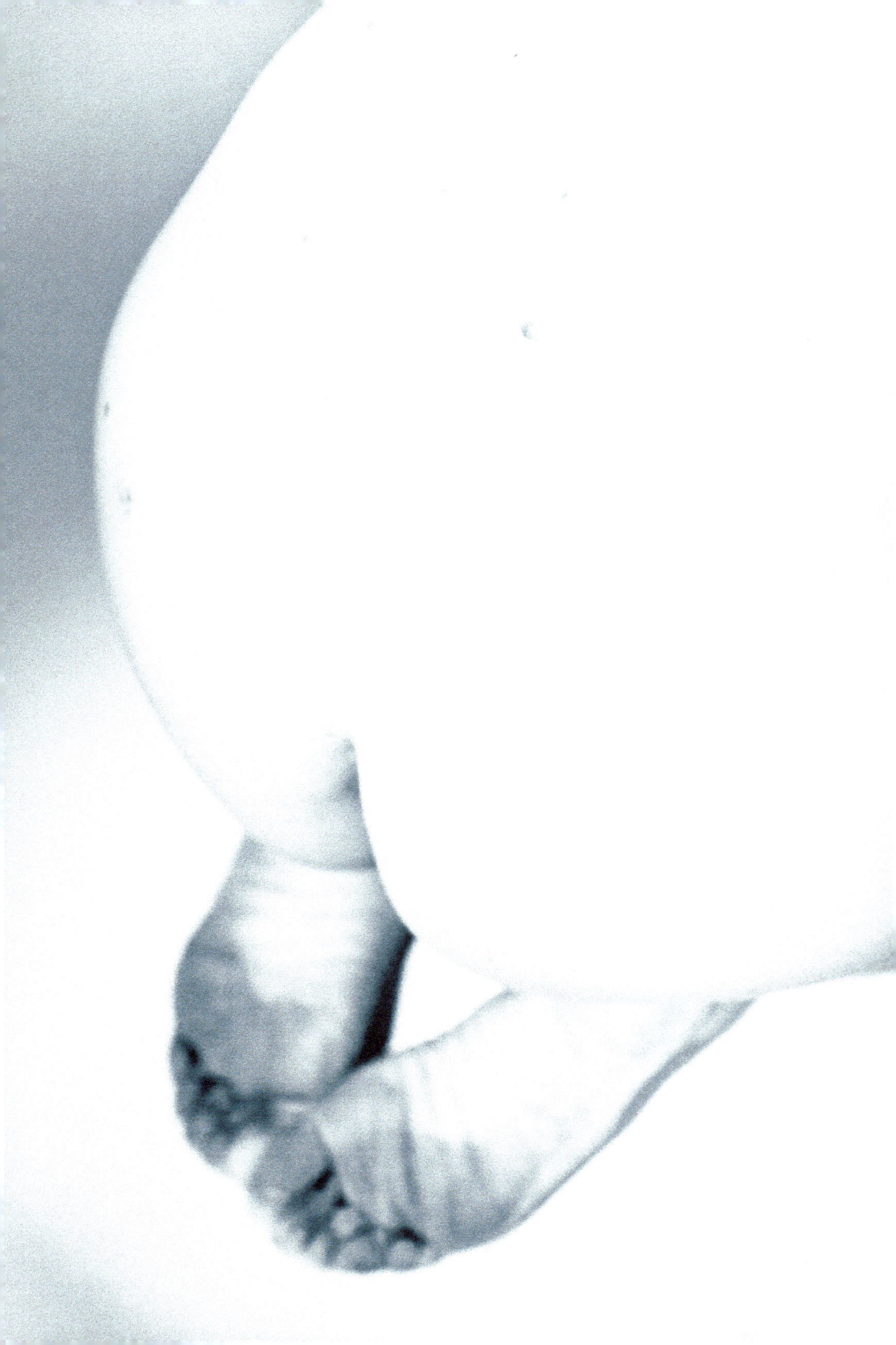

CARVED

today I wish to slice into each splay and spread of flesh
crossed in the afternoon the sole desire to press
two giant hams into shiny blade of steel or better still
to lay the curve of my convexity onto the cutting machine
excited by whirr and purr of possibility to remove
this subcutaneous bulge of buttered infidelity
squeezed between the grind of a gut grin glutton
punishment is sweeter than the feeding that precedes

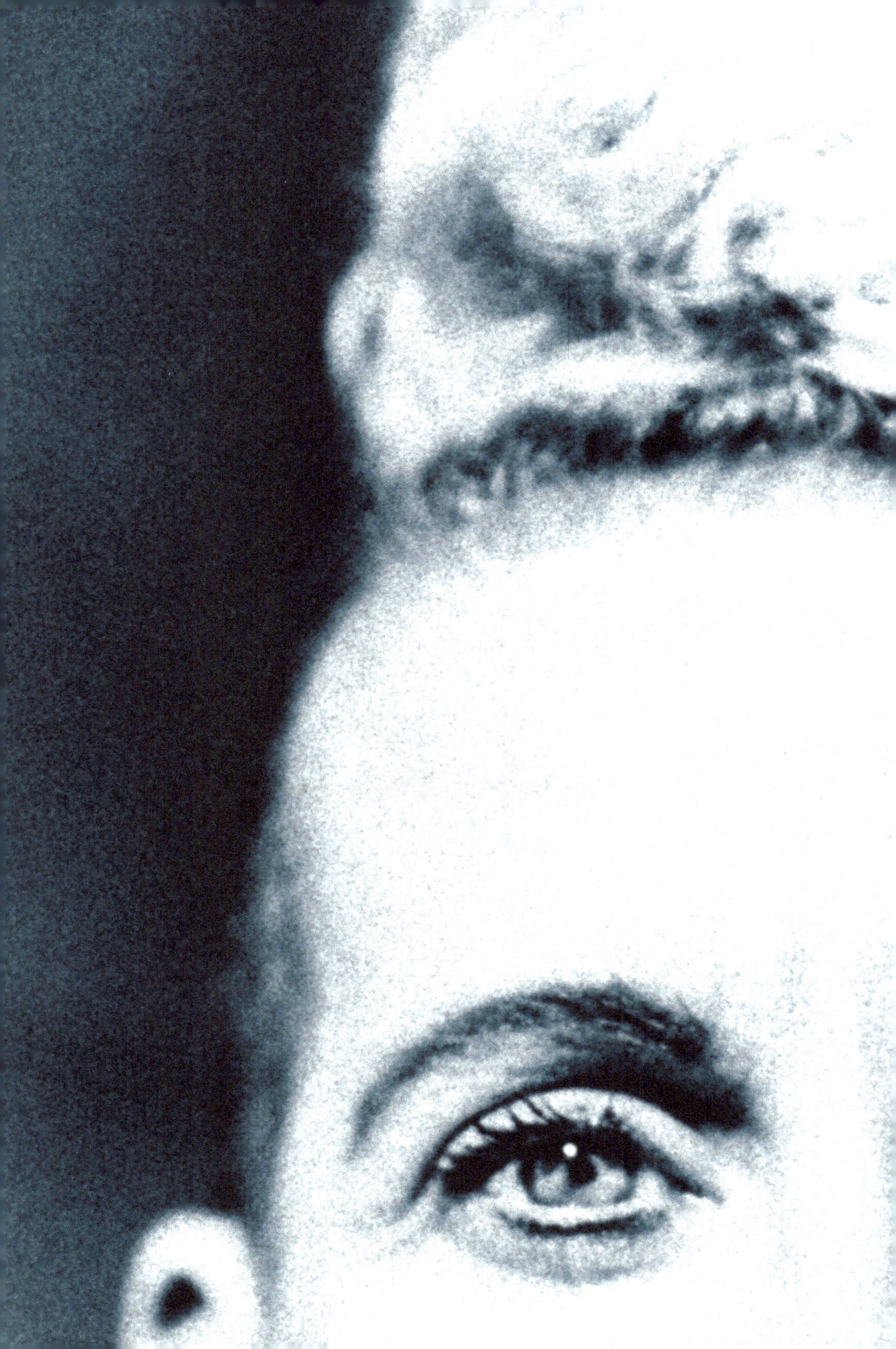

CATHARSIS

spinning into dusk
I catch a glance
at 4pm in the afternoon
a freakish high-haired clown
all-consuming – my rant
spitting bars into the impenetrable wall
that is your selfish surl
propellant arm whirl
of comedic desperation
wind-milling my utter despair
and desperation into the air
you have done it again
torturer teen
your incapacity to think
or feel or do anything
that makes even the tiniest sense
has incensed and sparked this flame
searing heart like a blacksmith
shoeing a lame horse – I surrender
your name emblazoned – smoking still
I fall like a cloth creature
into prostrate still-footed curve
exhausted doll at your feet
my nemesis – my dearest love – my defeat

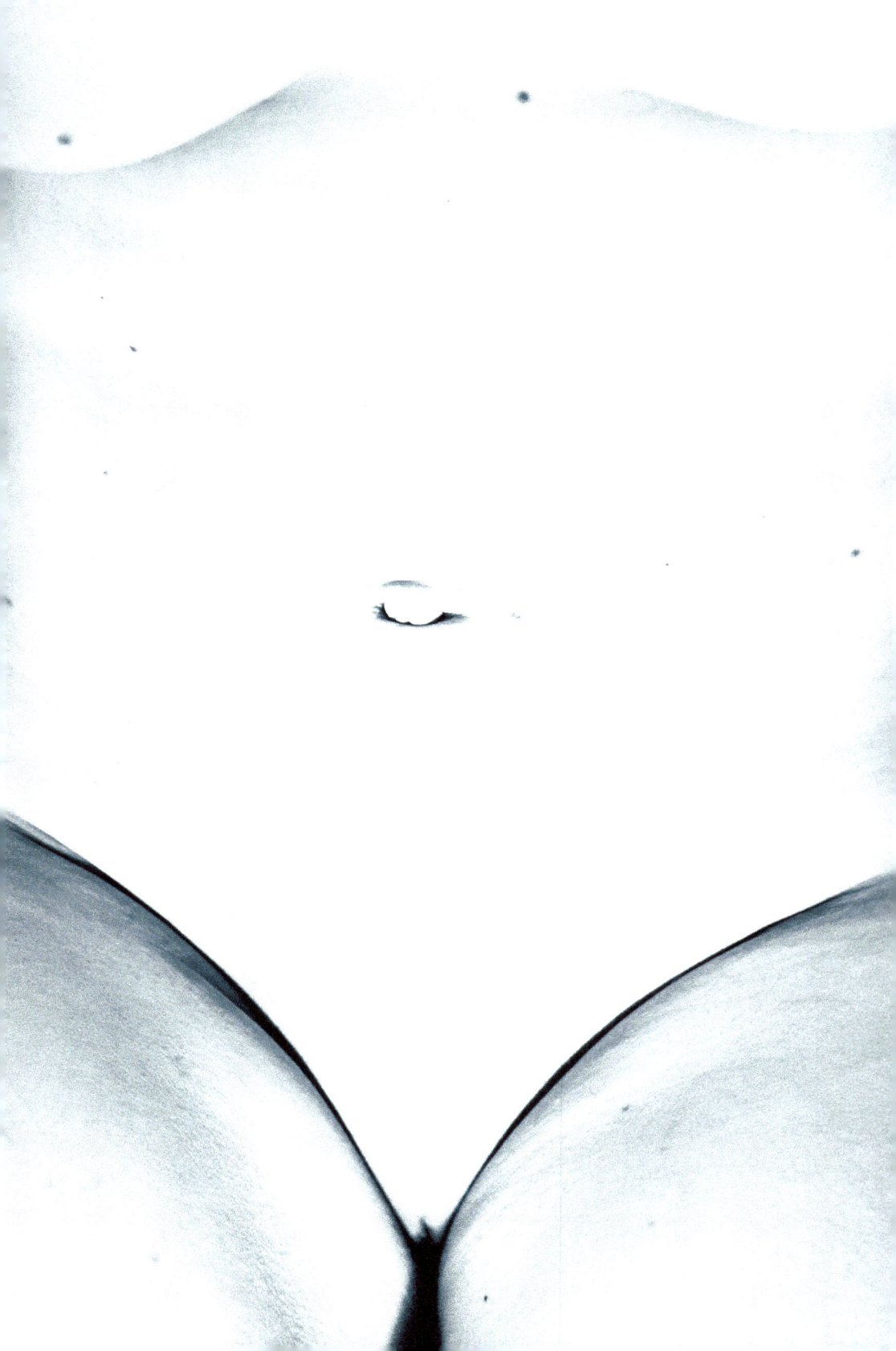

LADY V

All women have a tongue between their legs.
If mine could speak, then it would say,
Most probably, please go away.
In latter years she liquefies for few,
Has few friends and rarely speaks.
But when she does, the company she keeps
Is honoured to discover
Operatic diva – mother, lover.
Hard-won pearls of wisdom
Strung round fragile, swanlike frame.
Her name is herald,
Trumpeted from inner fortress
Moist with little sign of warring, birthing,
Battling for early-morning ribbed and spotted charms.
In calm serenity she basks, confident in knowledge that she is the soul
    of all.
No kiss and tell.
Although some hells have left their scars
Befitting chronic tales of males
Scrawling fetid messages indelibly, or so they thought,
On her poor stripped-bare toilet door.
She bleaches, teaches, scrubs and cleanses.
Menses swoosh and wash away
The bad man spunk of yesterday.
By night she sits, a regal queen,
An empress cushioned plumped in rose.
The door is closed to those who cannot satisfy,
Recoil at pink-tinged sunset sky,
Cannot abide the wilder stench of fish and eggs and death.
Who balk at rusted river flow and do not understand that
No means No is always No.
Give her space, unfettered time,
Free to stretch and burn in turn.
Sparingly permit her flight to outer labial realm.
For only one tongue has the key
To open up the inner she,
Crescendo reached in harmony.
She sings for you.
She sings for me.

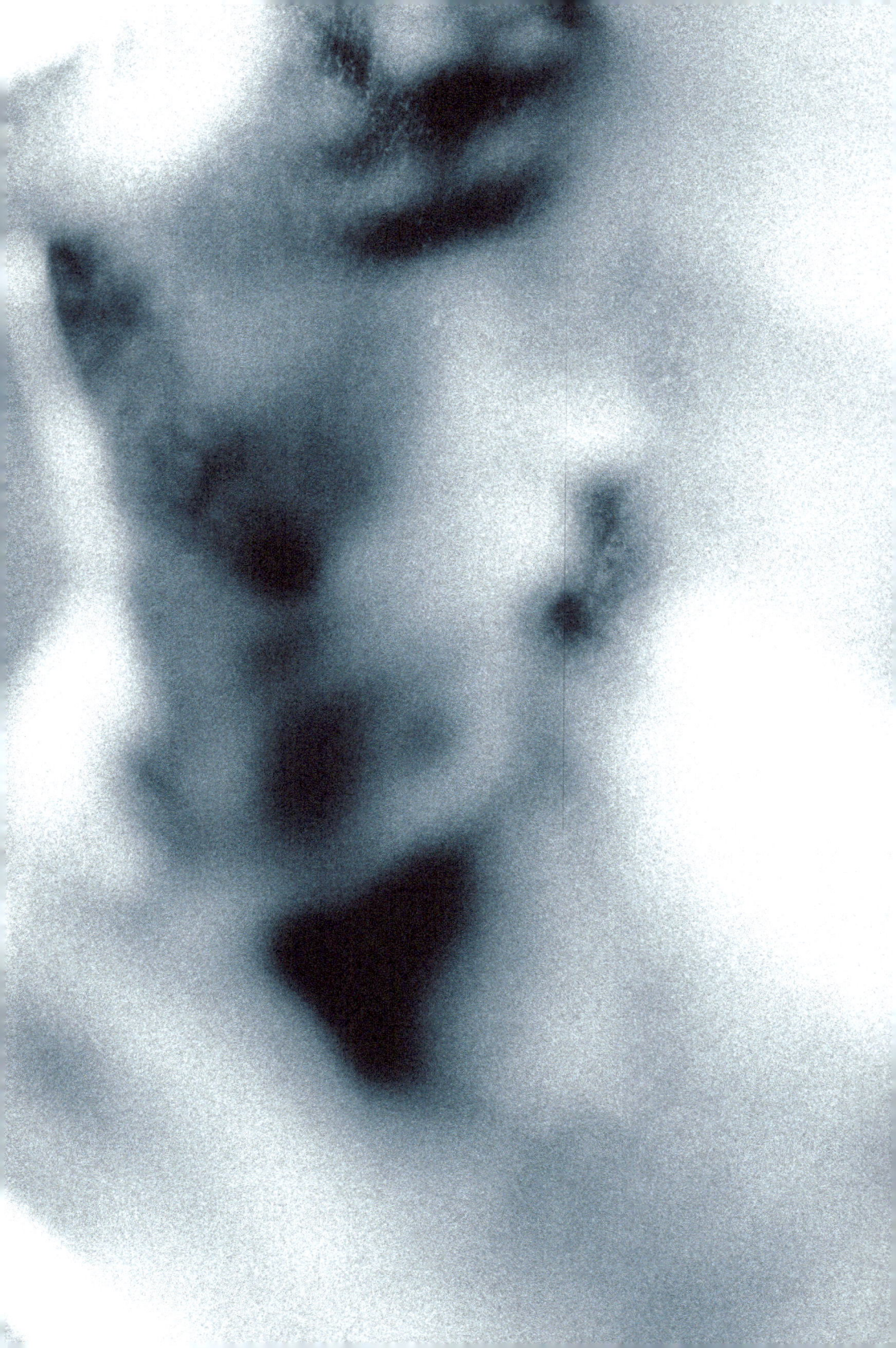

BONES

there are bones in my body I can only see
by midnight moon-spun light
the neat jut of scapula is to be admired
although I do have concerns about my neck
and if I lose any more will my age begin to show
as cheekbones resemble a hollow space below
the natural smile I used to break
before this awareness began
and hands expand to span
the waste in time it takes to wait
dismissal complete in a too-full plate
and counting is constant
the ticking and checking of fat content
avoidance takes over the day
with gum and cigarettes
and no thank you I just ate
as consciousness of all that I do not consume
is hammered home by nagging drone
sanctioning non-nourishment
berating all that is meant to be pleasant
sneaking away to measure
believing I am clever
in skipping meals that you create
there is no escape
as fork is raised to mouth
suddenly remembering
the washing that needs to be taken out
or something urgent in the other room
and doesn't the toilet smell bad again
reward of avoidance reveals itself
in mirrored trace of sinew taut
as spine and shoulders rise to drape
a sleekly skeletal shadow shape
subjugation is known control
and so, I win
knowing that this is sin
and yet I can never be
too thin

WATCHING THE BIRDS

Is this a sign of ageing?
Passive in sud-soaped task to rinse,
Wrist-dipped by servitude,
There is time, at least, to observe.
Spy each tiny wing-spanned curve.
The wilderness I have no time to tend
Has become their friend.
As one surviving rose
Stretches a slender neck, thrilling the breeze,
Below her knees all is industry.
Sparrows, finches,
Flock to pick and peck.
There is a formula to their forage, that we can never know.

I must be getting old.

QUATRAIN

Plummeting from darker skies,
Brothers in pillared wing,
Severing connected ties.
No longer shall they sing.

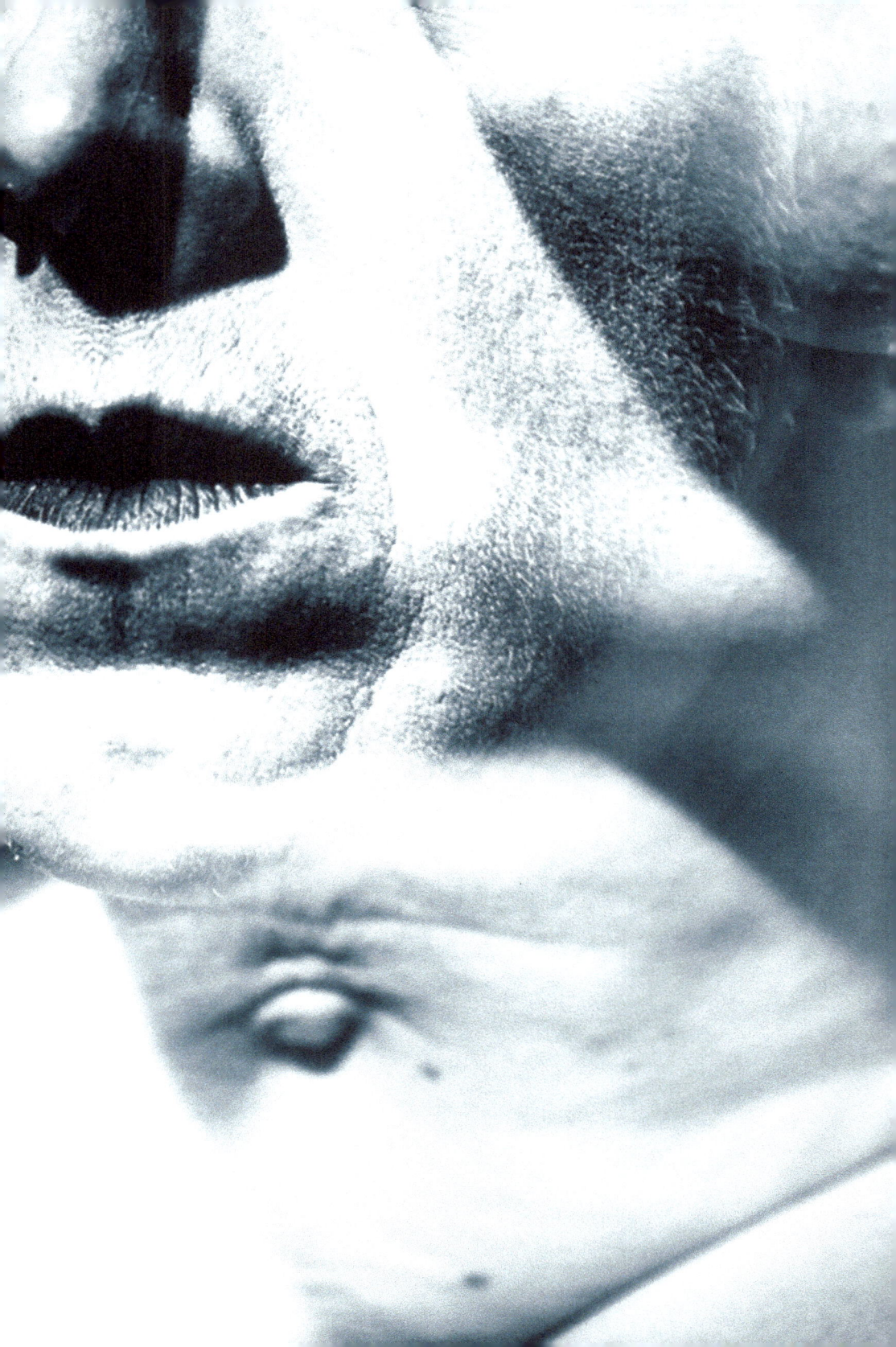

TEACHINGS OF THE FATHER

penetration is
the act or process of piercing
something
but more specifically
someone
and in the doing and knowing of this
aforementioned action
we are shown our place
face-down on occasion
we lie like twin bulbs
likening this inverted push
to the sound and howl
of a hyacinth

immobile in our atrophied
dismissal of skin
absorbing all the pain of the world
in silent acceptance
subservience is preternatural to our sex
and yet as purple bleeds into plum
the pummelling pleasure of it
ignites a new connection
and we forgive those
that trespass
holding closer
their innocence and inability
to stop

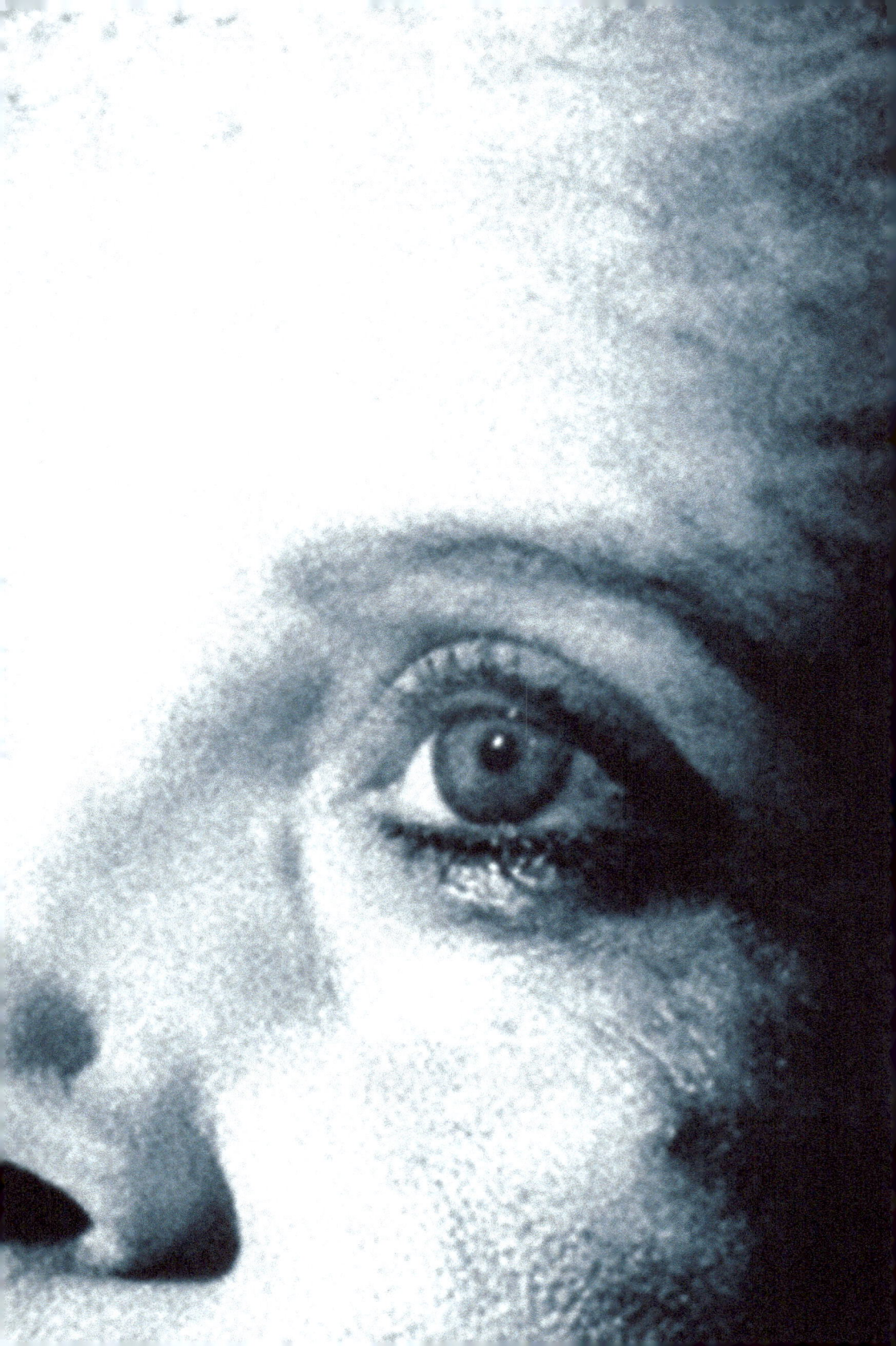

RUSH (ST MARY REDCLIFFE, 2012)

on the seventh day, under hot sweat canvas
we throw off the scent assaulting sense
thirsty yet galvanised by
hot post-rock-fest fizz
stuck now, inside a glittering peach
stone sucked dry, we lie
beached and bleached
primeval, clutched interrupted light frustrates
castrating a dream too heady to describe
we deep dive
sink into hatted river
rats swim close
bespectacled gentry – bent on being the best
plumed and groomed
muttered whispers weave and weft
attached to a brass band shuttle
solitary, soaring
we bow our sorry heads –
study the knitted hands of strangers
scented dowagers jostle for position
their rainbow posies strangulated by jugular green
we roll across the tides
yawn-driven vertigo
nauseating loss
at right angles
confessions
soothed by song
spewed, pewed
we defy
implode in gentle waiting
for time to release the rushes
their dry rasp
crisply out of context
under crunch-boned tread
the dead still sleep
encrypted
their code deciphered
as choral cohesion
answers all our prayers

EASTER SUNDAY

There are no eggs left
And the world is spare
As I wake, new in his resurrection,
To silent, childless numb.

The neighbours are strumming
Folk blue wanton wails.
As walls become thinner
I remember heightened nights.

When legs scrambled to twist,
Unfurling fingers, like newborn fists.
Stifling cries that children never hear
As they burrow deep for lost nuclear.

All the shops are closed
Aside from the crack converters
And the discount shoe store
With the outsize bargains.

The Pakistani man welcomes me
Into his hotchpotch shelving maze.
As the cheap deals bellow
I select two modest cans and leave.

REINCARNATION

in subterranean sea
blacker than light seal
stars have burnt their way
through the night
leaving an ink so thick
skeined vessels shrink to blink
lids lie dormant
unable to stretch limbs
singularly pliant, snaking
a psychedelic path to pain
spinal yellow bleeds into blue
amnesia is truly a blessing
in this eternity
evaporating depth
my horizontal ability
straining memory
as bubbled lungs
disintegrate
cells regroup
squirming for air
as one last gasp
completes me

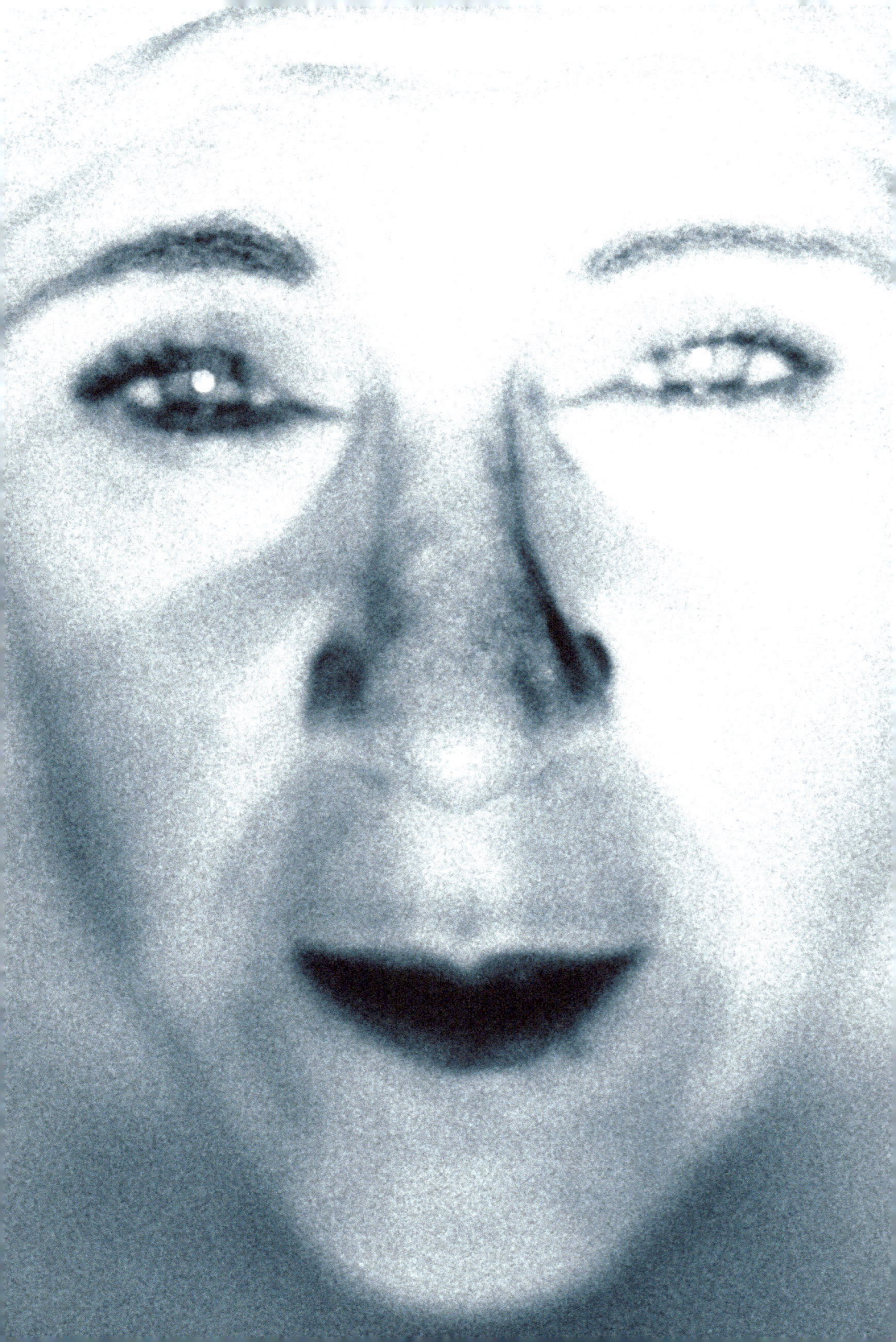

SCRAPED

higgledy piggledy
Raggedy Anns
nameless – we undress
mute children
in restraints
our maiden heads
green gowned
open fronted
bare footed
unvarnished toe
in sinking line
we hang
sorry vaginas
on belted hooks
blanketed clutch
marching pale
knees knock

flat backed
vein swell
masking indecision
we are gassed

blinded
by wounding
scraping, scooping
scarleteen scrawny necks

in triplicate
D&C dollies
we wake
we wake

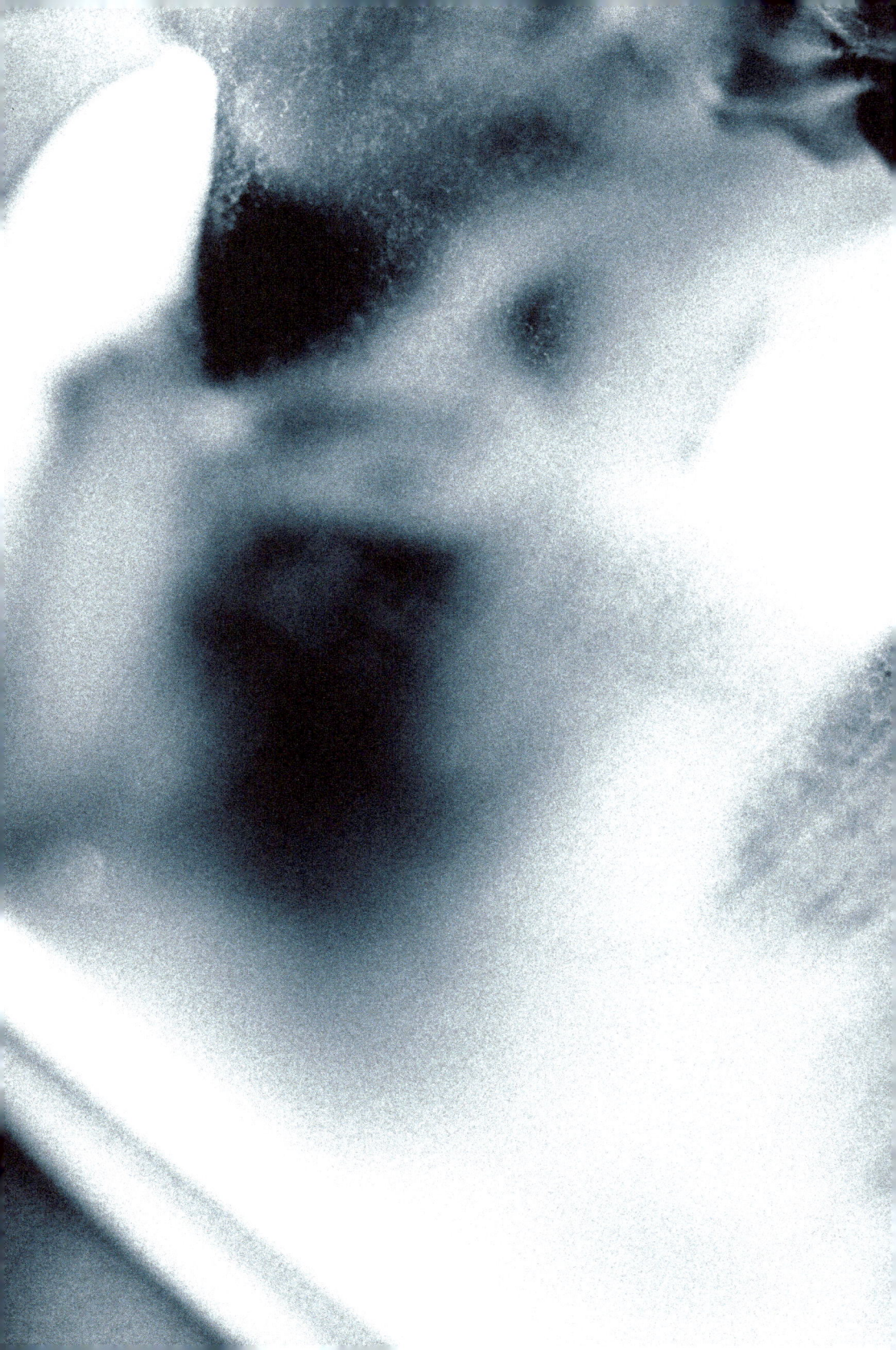

SCALP & SAUSAGE

You have no power.
In the late hour of itch
Cloaked in blue I stalk –
Blessing each chamber.
Imagining the bullet that belongs to you.
Violent male,
Brainless atrophy,
Another scalp laid bare.
Tragic trophy of a pointless affair.
Afraid of you?
I am not the first.
Let us lie together like sorry dolls,
My sisters and I.
Ragged, split by a too-tight fist.
What happened?
Did the real one let you down?
Back to the dolls' house you prowl.
Reach in to squeeze another gentle neck.
I play dead.
Perhaps not dead enough.
I cook meat in my oven.
Savour the ulcerated stench.
It reminds me of you.
Pig gut.
Fat fuck.
Flesh is warm and ready.
You are chewed.
Eaten and consumed.
Spit-stained gristle picked from teeth.
The ritual affords momentary relief.

FRAGMENTS OF A DAY (ONE VOICE)

Dream-sucked, we wake.
Skin on skin on skin.
What lies between us and this day
But a nail-scratched hair glue shirt?
Silent in our pact.
A solid wall of nothingness.
Drowning out the tiny heartbeat.
Admitting defeat.
We rise to wash the guilt from adult pores.
In four hours you will be no more.
Concrete vows cemented by a shared agreement that this is
    absolutely the right thing to do.
I love you.
Grey-flaked.
I am not permitted to eat.
Nil by mouth, they said.
Odd, the taste that has become metallic nemesis.
Spreading – coating dumb lump flesh.
You are sheepish in your swallowing.
We do not speak of biscuits.
Or natural emetics.
Not today.
Overcast for August.
Summer is remiss.
Late to her own party.
Train coming. Train coming.
We cannot be tardy.
Hazy pin-punched numbers purchase ticketed ride to seaside divide.
We arrive.
Plaited by tears from a goodbye stranger.
Following the radar into blue we stalk.
Remember to talk.
Hands clasped, twisting.
Steep hill arrow points to sky bridge.
Curling, curling, upward swirling we ascend.
Myself and best friend.
I consider jumping.
Throwing myself into the arms of a high-speed hurtling angel.
Anything but face the clinical anonymity of a residential butcher.
Killing time. Killing time.

Walking in silent Edwardian Blyton avenue.
Tiptoe, tiptoe.
We dare not wake the neighbours.
Draw attention to imminent crime.
Black-coated, flat-footed.
I despise your maleness.
Question your very being.
Unfair and inappropriate.
WHO ARE YOU?
Your answer hits the air and falls to curl like a kitten's tongue around my heart.
A flawed man who has made a mistake.
Another one. Or is it two?
We embrace.
I kiss your worried, careworn face.
Walk to door. Hesitant.
Each step taking us closer.
Buzzer pressed.
We enter a chav-packed haze of eager victims.
Chattering silently.
All teeth. No gums.
My throat expands.
Tightening ready for flight.
Upstairs it is empty.
Thankful we sink into leather.
A clipboard distracts with demands for personal information.
Date of birth. Next of kin
The irony that it is still him.
I cannot remember your phone number.
If I die, who will you tell?
I am going to hell anyway.
Women come and go.
Catherine. Who? Oh, yes.
Catherine. Me. Me.
Who is me?
Room is small.
Smaller than me.
Smaller than it.
Smaller than the answer.
Are you sure? Are you sure?

If you're not sure we may not be able to, may not be able to, may not be able to.
Get a grip. Remember the task in hand.
Show no fear. You are here.
I am black. Tiny. Plain-clothed.
Coral-tipped, pitying.
Her perfect nails mock.
My hands are stripped.
A bride in preparation for a pact.
Nakedly rigid and ready to burn.
Tissues are in evidence.
Medically I am sound.
That's good.
Psychologically, perhaps not.
Returning to lilac chamber, plaited woman has reappeared.
I whisper. You respond. Acknowledge her.
From the station earlier.
In tears, she grips onto a man she cannot have.
Courage dripping through her legs like an incontinent sow.
Poor cow. Poor cow.
Moo. Moo.
Bovine we bond.
Plaited woman is with meditating friend.
I am summoned to room number two by a nurse.
I am Jackie, she smiles.
Inside starched blue – the voice is kinder.
This is my trainee assistant, she says.
Is it OK if she stays?
No, it is not OK.
Not OK.
But I do not say.
Removing trousers, knickers, I am laid on paper.
A wasted feast for the medics.
They are checking for signs of life.
I steel myself to turn away.
The cold jelly shivers.
Evidence is secured.
Knickers knocking next to knees.
Herded back to the lilac.

You look up as I enter.
We move downstairs.
Back to the chav chatter.
At the door – a chaste goodbye.
I cross from emerald into monochrome.
A child in the hands of a speculum.

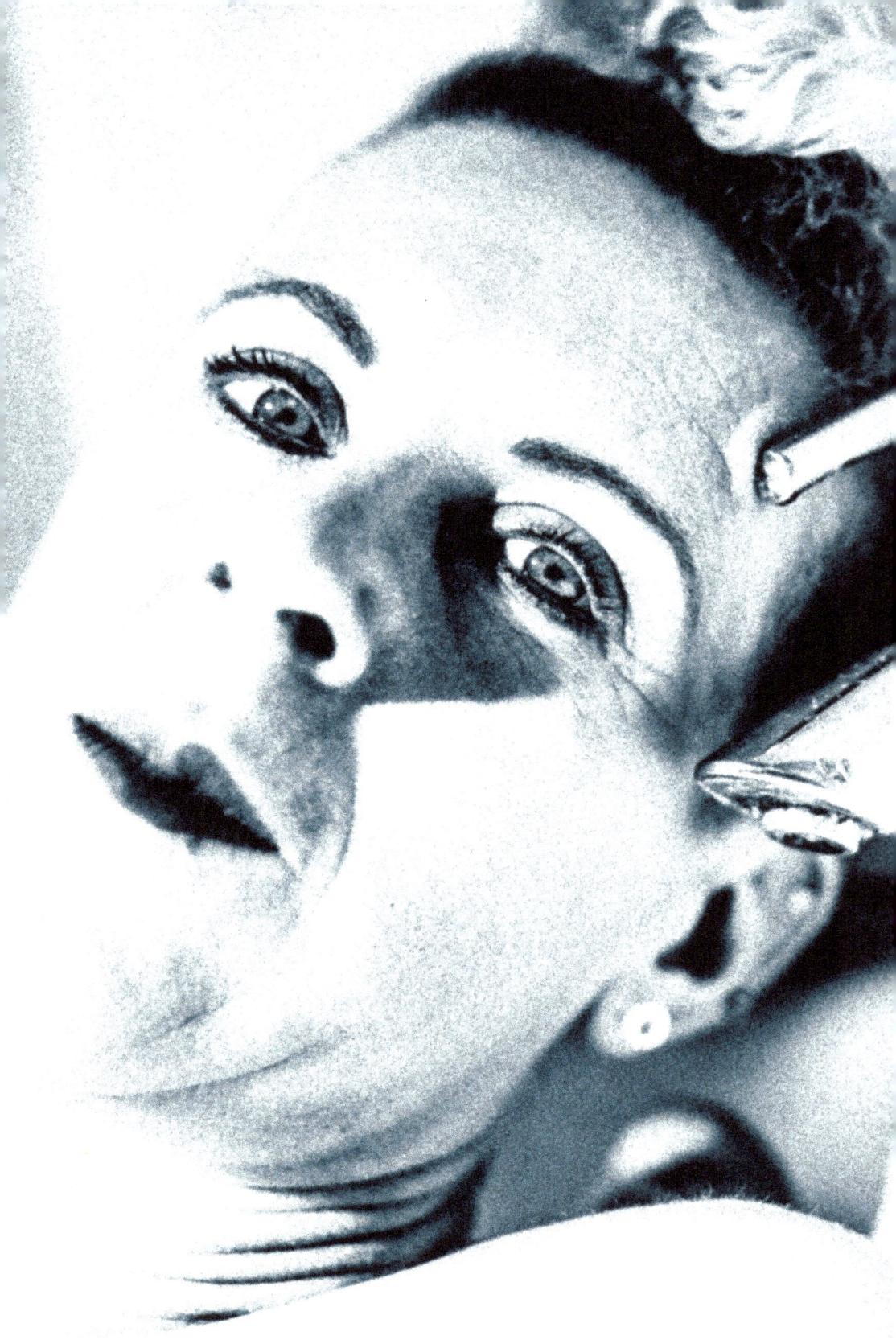

TRISTESSE

lie with me a little
in this outer space of otherness
long after stars have melted their light
into eponymous core
and the blood beat buzz
of the head banger boogie
subsides into steady 4/4
permission is granted
to unwind these hooks
unnetting – the catch
has been abundant
as ears uncleave from chest
untugging lips to sink
the we-made flesh separates
crawling to regain its shape
as a new creature stalks the shadow
limping away to nestle
stroking its joyless joy

KEYHOLE

the neighbour is crying
her weighted whelps
seep through the wall
as I discover
the old silver clock
in a forgotten drawer
and sneak
to slide a battery
into plastic void
resetting time
the tick of empty
recalibrates tomorrow
as I – her neighbour
rock in time
to her sorrow

COLD SHOULDER

beaten
I crawl
to the end of us
lay my thin frame
on the edge of the world
praying for axis to tip
as shoulder grazes
the sting of you
repellent
skim-rimmed by tired
eyes pinned into salt-smudge black
stapled to the sky
we can never return
to earth

SOUP 1 (NEW YEAR'S DAY)

Since early dawn, a tailored trail of misshapen vegetables have passed through your square-end blunted thumbs.
Chopped and splayed into regular, stewing in a new juice born of chicken and orange root.
Steam-fugged, shifting from foot to foot, quelling desire to wipe your ceramic splattered gloop.
Pyjama owls – anointing our tongues in climactic first foot soup.

SOUP 2 (FOUR YEARS EARLIER)

Curled in a thinner frame, I straddle the afternoon, calling out the
    newness of your name,
Hold sound tight in throat until breath can no longer bear witness to this
    sudden rush of blood and bite.
Rocking tight – a shared skin punctures all as white light strikes and falls.
I am fearful of rain and the residue that may drip slowly into sockets.
The soup bubbles ever higher, as rising steam obliterates the shared
    sticky residue.

You will learn not to tell me everything.

GHERKINS

When I am unhappy, I do not eat.
And my body refuses to smile
Or lift its skin into the light.
The fight to allow breath is
Involuntary dysfunction
As chest adopts an unknown arrhythmic swagger,
Beating its hammer head on the bone
Of a penalty and legacy of another.

I remember days of singular gherkins.
Sucked by the sun. Offered as treats
As he reached to stroke new pony legs.
Before fucking white thinness on a concrete dusty floor.
Next to his cupboard, overflowing with brown-lipped people.
Naked and raw – I had never seen chicken-skin cunts before.

Later – in icy cold – I sluice soiled softness,
Rinsing away emetic cum in a handheld chrome surround.
Scraping silent tongue clean of falseness.
His psychosis imprinted
In the sheets and lines of my face
As waif-wan thighs collect new tattoos,
Fist-shaped and purple.

The man downstairs has turned his music louder.

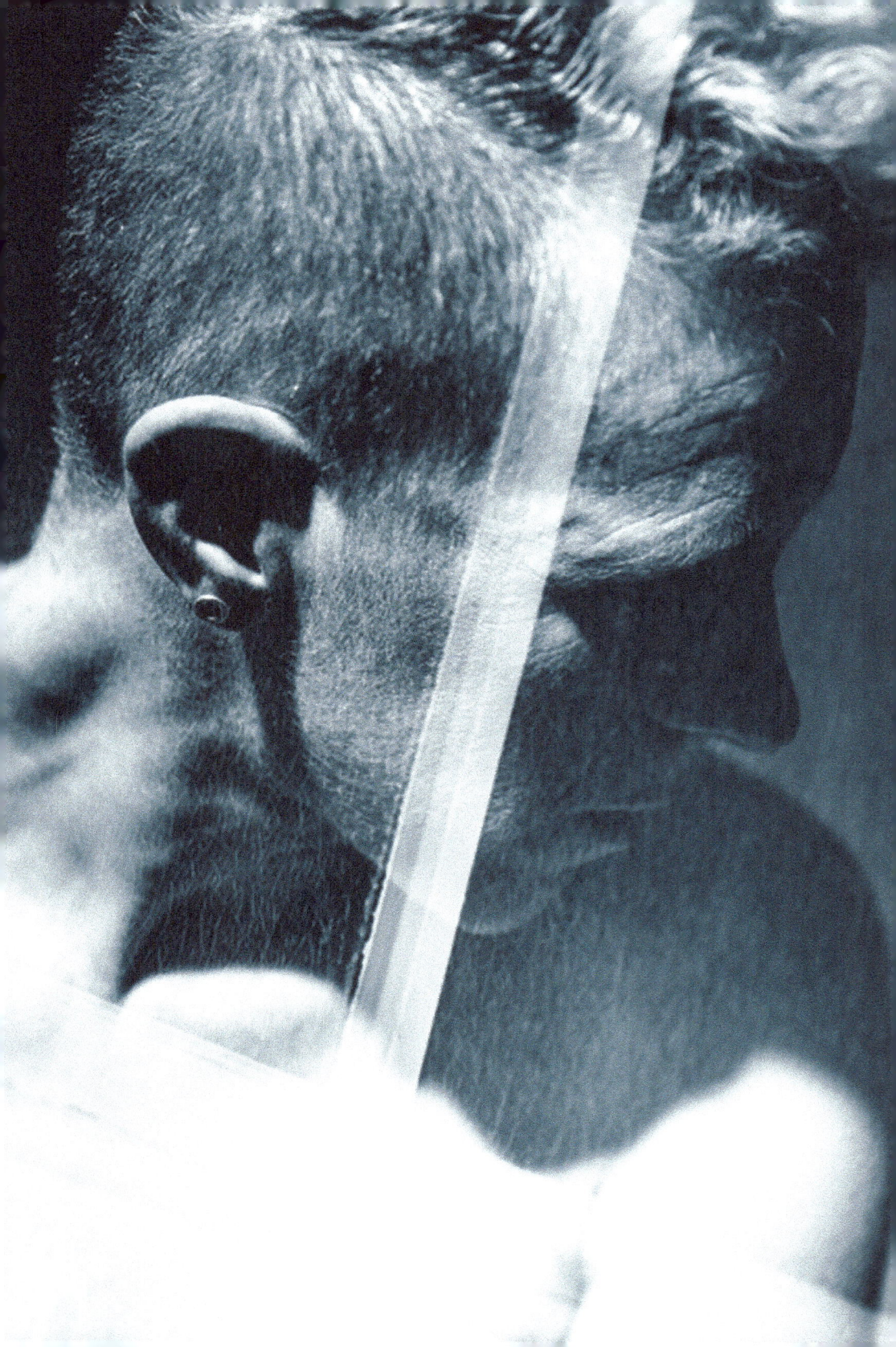

PUNK SKY (STOKES CROFT)

tonight
a wild Mohican
has painted the sky
her high hair
scraping its altitude
onto chalk-green clouds
pink guts
spill into ribbons
lacing the boots of a lost night
we are kicked
bruised and laughing
into the afterglow –
unapologetic and free.

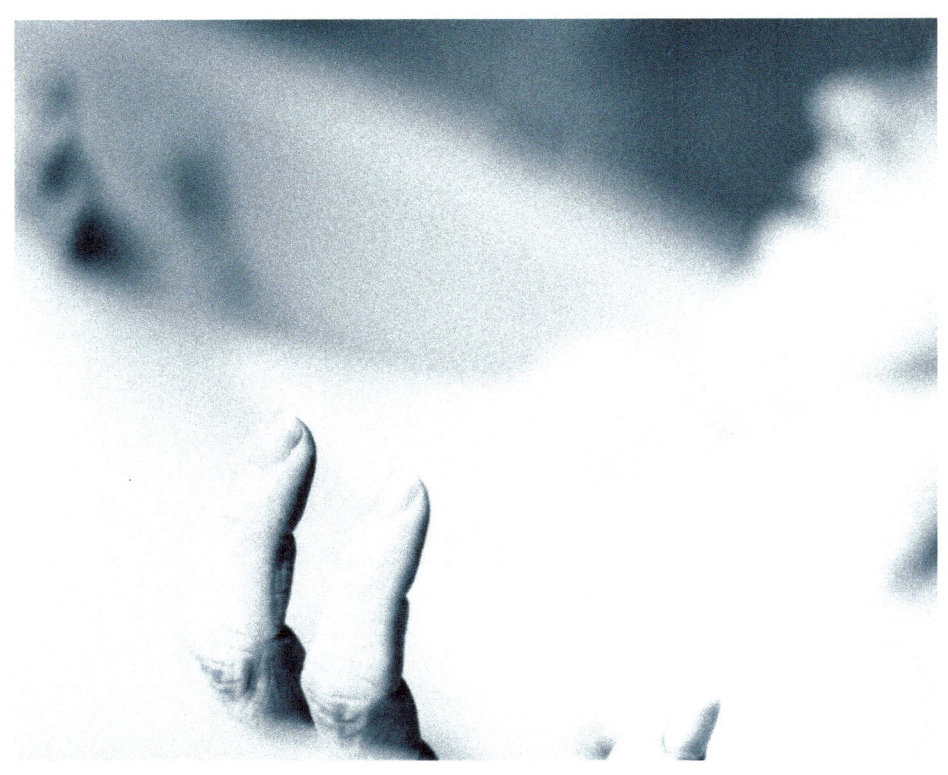

ARBORETUM

under maple skies, leaves wince
shield their faces from the sun
today we are not cruel – not today
rather we follow the Buddha
his banyan tree provides shelter
as paths fork into yew-dark dreams
the berries rain in vertical lines
we notate the branches
peer to scribble their Latin names
we do not have a dog still

TOMB

in this space – we rest
a seamless skin
our lineage altered

under wet felt
heavy dew wakes

by beaded diamond pools
we see again

blind sockets
damp with tears

symbiotic
worm-riddled

you laugh at my decay
we are the same

eternity, a riddle solved
we wasted so much
on so little

relieved
ribs rubbing
we collapse into dust

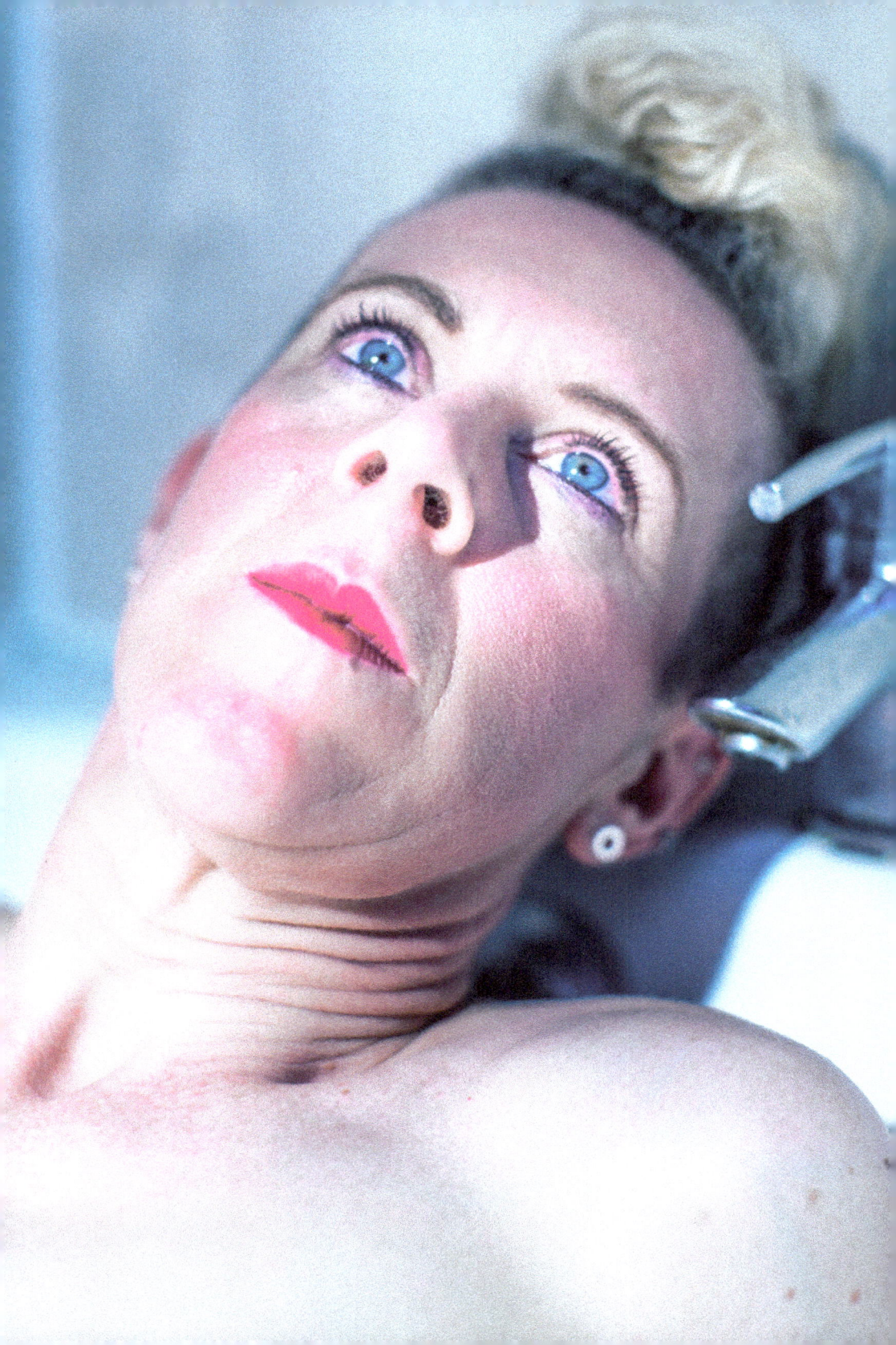

BRANCHES OF SKY

You lie.
Your head over mine.
Weight bearing down.
Entwined in embrace with no escape.
Softly, slowly, you wrap around me
These branches of sky.
I smell pepper, spices, essence of earth.
Red, green and gold.
Scents of an ancient world, a time when lions roared.
Now no more.
I cry.
Not for myself.
Not for you.
I cry for the peace of the moment.
The dark, stillness of calm.
Inside, deep inside, another listens and waits.
Their time now.

ACKNOWLEDGEMENTS

Dad: For genetic gifts of soul and sensitivity.
Mum: For your indomitable spirit.
Grandma: For your unconditional love.
Siblings: Andy, Simon, Emma & Ami for shared genes.
Lovers: Known and unknown.
Abusers: Known and unknown.

Claudio Ahlers for capturing my deepest self.

To my varied, vibrant and wonderful families and friends – by extension, connection and/or separation – thanks to fate, divine intervention, luck or otherwise. You know who you are.

Jo Bell for advice and belief.
Mike Manson for more belief and mentorship.
Alan Summers for haiku and brevity.
John Siddique and Andrew Macmillan.
Burning Eye for trusting my truth and making it tangible.

And finally, thank you to experience and bad decisions.
Without scars we are unblemished statues.
To bleed, to endure, to heal is to become human.

Lightning Source UK Ltd.
Milton Keynes UK
UKHW02f1012040918
328262UK00009BA/200/P